Improve Your Memory

To my wife Zoe for your inspiration and belief, you are my lucky star

And for my three boys Zachery, Elijah and Noah, whose creativity and fun knows no bounds.

Improve Your Memory

Mark Channon

First published in Great Britain in 2011 by Hodder Education.

This edition published in 2016 by John Murray Learning

Copyright © Mark Channon 2011, 2016

The right of Mark Channon to be identified as the Author of the Work has been asserted by him in accordance with the Copyright, Designs and Patents Act 1988.

Database right Hodder & Stoughton (makers)

The *Teach Yourself* name is a registered trademark of Hachette UK.

British Library Cataloguing in Publication Data: a catalogue record for this title is available from the British Library.

ISBN 9781473613515

eISBN 9781473613522

1

The publisher has used its best endeavours to ensure that any website addresses referred to in this book are correct and active at the time of going to press. However, the publisher and the author have no responsibility for the websites and can make no guarantee that a site will remain live or that the content will remain relevant, decent or appropriate.

The publisher has made every effort to mark as such all words which it believes to be trademarks. The publisher should also like to make it clear that the presence of a word in the book, whether marked or unmarked, in no way affects its legal status as a trademark.

Every reasonable effort has been made by the publisher to trace the copyright holders of material in this book. Any errors or omissions should be notified in writing to the publisher, who will endeavour to rectify the situation for any reprints and future editions.

Typeset by Cenveo® Publisher Services.

Printed and bound in Great Britain by CPI Group (UK) Ltd., Croydon, CR0 4YY.

John Murray Learning policy is to use papers that are natural, renewable and recyclable products and made from wood grown in sustainable forests. The logging and manufacturing processes are expected to conform to the environmental regulations of the country of origin.

Carmelite House
50 Victoria Embankment
London EC4 0DZ
www.hodder.co.uk

Contents

Acknowledgements

My thanks to Jonathan Shipley, Victoria Roddam, Helen Rogers, Althea Brooks, Antonia Maxwell and everyone at John Murray Learning for the opportunity and support; Phil Poole for his last minute, tasty recipe; Stephen Mear for choreography that I still remember and can talk about after ten years.

There have been several people in one way or another who have shaped my thinking around memory. Thanks to the unstoppable Steve Rogers for introducing me to the world of memory techniques in the early '90s; Mel Gordon for a book that influenced my early days as an actor and informed my ideas around memory improvement; James E. Zull for writing a book that made a shift in my approach to training and coaching; Tony Buzan for his early and ongoing inspiration in the area of Mind Maps; Anthony Robbins for his strategies that have created massive change many times throughout my life.

Thanks to everyone who offered the use of their photos and the ones we were able to print: Cola Richmond, Alison Shepherd, Carol Williams, Caroline Marsden, Emmalene Evans, John Norris, John Pasonage, Joseph Pitcher, Nathan Amzi (contact@ amziphotography.co.uk), Tom Kershaw, Mark Stuart, Rebecca Thornhill, John Barr, Rebecca Lock, Steven O'Neill, Lorraine Chappell, Dermot Keaney, Stephen McCarthy and Nick Brownlow (with an extra thanks to Nick for his help with research).

Thanks to Mum and Dad for their never-ending belief in all my endeavours; John and Paul for their constant support; and I have to mention Dominic for the couple of conversations that got me going – you know who you are.

With special thanks to my wife Zoë for her unparalleled support, research, ability to appear interested at 3am and invaluable motivation throughout the writing of this book.

Meet the author

It is fair to say that in my youth, I would not have been regarded as having the best memory. After training as an actor in the late 1980s I always felt fairly comfortable learning scripts; however, trying to retain names, facts and semantic knowledge was more of a challenge.

It wasn't until my early 20s after a good friend of mine, Steve Rogers, loaned me a memory course that I had what you might call 'a light bulb moment'. I have seen the exact same reaction from hundreds of people since, the thought slowly forming in their brain, working its way down to their mouth before blurting out, 'Why did no one teach me this at school?'. I was hooked; however, I wanted to do more than just remember lists, I was hungry to find out where I could apply these techniques in my life.

Around a year later while working in the West End production of *Crazy for You*, I had an interesting call from my agent asking if I had any good ideas for a game show. Being an actor, you never say no: 'Let me think about it and get back to you.' This seemed like an opportunity and within 30 minutes I wrote a format for a game show called *Memory Masters*: ordinary people from all walks of life performing incredible memory feats after attending an intensive memory seminar. Within one week of posting it off, I pitched to a production company, and in 12 months it was a weekly prime time show on the BBC, presented by Bob Monkhouse.

This started my journey as a trainer and coach in the world of memory techniques and mind mapping. Over the course of the next year, I came sixth in the World Memory Championships and was ranked third in the world as a Grand Master of Memory. My focus, however, was not so much on competition but on where these techniques could add value in a person's life.

Over the last 20 years, as well as being an actor, hypnotherapist and coach, I have run seminars for organizations such as Rothschild, Lincoln National, Dyslexia Scotland, the Institute of

Chartered Accountants for England and Wales and the BBC in Memory, Mind Mapping and Creativity; worked with students of all ages and trained at many top independent schools in the UK such as Eton, Roedean, Oakham, Woldingham, Oundle, St Bede's, Whitgift and St Peter's (York); and over the last five years worked to deliver digital products for the BBC, Microsoft (Skyped), *The Telegraph* and most recently the role of Chief Digital Officer for RouteMap (http://theroutemap.com) helping students build skills and evidence for university

My passion and experience across a mix of careers have allowed me to pull together simple and highly effective strategies in *Improve Your Memory* that are focused on helping you progress your career and identify ways of using the ancient art of memory techniques in order to add real value to your life, be that for business or leisure.

At the core of *Improve Your Memory* is the 'idea' not just to remember but to remember with a purpose and not just to understand but to take action and get results.

I have been lucky enough over the years to teach these strategies to students and professionals of all ages and it is truly exciting to have the privilege of sharing these strategies with you.

Mark Channon

www.memoryschool.com

Introduction

Interestingly, in the beginning I never really considered myself a 'memory guy', memory techniques were part of what I did. While I enjoyed the process of training to a high standard, competing in various championships and experiencing first-hand the positive impact that these techniques can have in many areas of your life, for me, memory improvement was always a means to an end. I think that sentiment still runs true and it is why I have been passionate about sharing the ideas in this book.

There have been many memory improvement books written over the years and I have read quite a few of them. When starting out, the thing that I looked for in most of those books was examples, 'How do I put this into practice?' This was a challenge and although there were some excellent books that gave a great insight into how memory techniques worked, I always felt there wasn't enough guidance in real-world application and enough to chew on that would allow me to immerse myself so it became second nature.

Having an eclectic background and various careers (dancer, actor, developer, trainer, coach, product manager), it always seemed clear to me that to really understand something you have to experience it and take some form of *action*, to master something you have to immerse yourself in it. Through that mastery you can perform at a high level and create the changes you are looking for in your life.

I wanted to learn how to improve my memory so I could learn scripts more quickly for auditions, understand programming when I started developing websites back in the late 1990s, memorize names in meetings, remember key facts about people, consume information from conferences, put together presentations and memorize them at high speed, programme myself to remember things at a specific moment in time – the list goes on.

Almost from the very beginning I was so excited about what was possible I couldn't help but talk to people about these amazing techniques and try to figure out how memory techniques could help them.

To that end the learning strategies and memory techniques throughout this book will take you on a journey from understanding and experiencing through immersion in the techniques to choosing how you can apply it to mastery in your own career.

This journey has four destinations:

▶ **Foundations** – The ideas you learn in this section will set you up for how to approach the strategies throughout the rest of the book.

▶ **A new way of thinking** – This is your toolkit; here you will learn your craft.

▶ **How to remember** – An opportunity to immerse yourself in the application of these strategies.

▶ **Become an expert in your field** – Make an real impact in your career or business, bringing these skills to your everyday life.

The book is packed full of '**Try it now**' boxes. When you see a 'Try it now' box you should switch from passive reading to active participation; this will increase your understanding and memory of the chapter as well as your ability to look for opportunities for where to apply the strategy or concept in your own life. All 'Try it now' boxes have a **Time limit**: this is the set time for each exercise. While some can be completed more quickly and some take longer, the time limit constrains the amount of time you spend on each 'Try it now' to make sure you keep the momentum up through the book. Everyone is different so these are a rough guide. If you find you haven't completed a 'Try it now' within the time limit, either come back to it later or run the time limit again.

Depending on your mode at the time, you may choose to do the 'Try it now' exercises as you go through the book and treat it as a training session or make notes on the exercises that capture your interest and come back to these later. Even if you feel a 'Try it now' exercise isn't particularly relevant, you should read through and think about where you may apply this in your own life.

Try one now: each 'Try it now' consists of a short game or exercise to complete.

Try it now: Your purpose
Time limit: 10 minutes

* Without thinking too hard, answer these questions (if you have a pen and paper, write them down):
  ▷ Why are you reading this book?
  ▷ What do you want to get from it?
* If you haven't done so already – preview this book (take no more than five minutes); flick through and get a sense of what it's about. Certain areas will catch your attention: notice these but don't focus on remembering them.
* Make sure you do the above steps before reading on.
* Make a few notes about anything you remember that caught your attention, this could be as few as one or two things or as many as 20.

You already have the potential to remember anything you put your mind to. Since you are reading this book you are probably looking for ways to improve your current ability to remember or get some practical ideas about how it can help you in your everyday life, business or career.

Some of you may only want to become competent, extracting the key techniques that will allow you to do specific tasks. Others may want to go deeper, acquiring the ability to become effective on a personal level and use the techniques in your career.

You may want to achieve a level of expertise or mastery that is integrated throughout your life, where you no longer think in terms of techniques but it's just what you do, how you learn, how you act and how you lead others.

There is no magic wand and although you will be able to memorize more quickly, remember more and retain it for longer, like any skill, expertise takes time and dedication.

The aim of this book is not to give a detailed view on 'how your brain works' but rather to offer you memory techniques and learning strategies that will add real value in your life and in your career or business. The intention is not to have you remember 'everything' you read or have done but to offer you the skills to remember 'anything' you put your mind to.

Memory techniques are very personal and will be interpreted in many different ways. Your goal should be to take what you read here, experience it and make it your own.

Whichever path you choose, the strategies in this book can help you make a difference in your life and your career. Have fun and enjoy the journey!

Part One

Foundations

'Efforts and courage are not enough without purpose and direction.'

John F. Kennedy

1

Memory

In this chapter you will learn:

- ▶ *the importance of memory for you*
- ▶ *the most common types of memory that people refer to*
- ▶ *the building blocks of memory*
- ▶ *about the art of memory.*

The purpose of this chapter is not to give a detailed view of the brain but to let you reflect on the importance of memory in your life, the various types of memory you may be familiar with and your own capability. By making a 'shift' in your perception and therefore your beliefs about what is possible, you can start to unblock any pre-conceived ideas about the practical uses of memory techniques.

Your memory

It seems that in our current world, where we are expected to remember more and more, there should be more focus on not just the 'what we remember' but also the 'how to remember'. We spend years learning to read and write and months or years learning to play a sport, but when it comes to learning, and specifically to learning techniques that can help with this, the commitment can be minimal. This may be because those techniques are not readily available at the right time or there could be a presumption that it wastes time or it's easier just to press on; maybe there is a belief that it's how you are wired: 'You can remember this but can't remember that.'

Key idea: Mastering your memory

Memory is an art and like any other art it takes time to master; like most things you master, the benefits can be great. The trick is figuring out what level of expertise you need to get to in order to achieve your goals. How good do you need and want your memory to be? To answer those questions you need to identify how your memory currently helps or hinders you in your life.

Try it now: Memory in your life
Time limit: 10 minutes

We all inherently know that memory is vital in order to function; without memory we have no understanding or context. Answer the questions below to identify your strengths and weaknesses:

* What frustrates you most about your memory?
* Where does your memory perform well?
* If you have used memory techniques before, how successful were they?
* If you have used memory techniques before, what was the biggest challenge?
* What do you expect to be able to do after reading and working through the actions in this book?
* On a scale of 1–10, how would you rate your current memory?
* On a scale of 1–10, where would you like your memory to be?
* What does 1 look like for you and what does 10 look like?
* Make a note of your scores and put it somewhere visible.
Try the online survey at
http://improve-your-memory.memoryschool.com

Memory types

There are lots of different terms used to describe various types of memory. Our aim is not to give an account of all the different memory types and meanings, or whether one term should be used over the other, but rather to give an overview of some basic terms in use, giving you some context as to where or how you might experience them. This pragmatic approach will give us a common language to refer to.

Key idea: Types of memory

Concise Learning and Memory (John H. Byrnes, 2009), references the fact that Tulving (2007) identified 256 types of memory.

EXPLICIT (CONSCIOUS) MEMORY

With explicit memory there is a conscious effort to recollect, whether you are thinking about a past experience or some type of factual information.

Try it now: Study the following words

Time limit: 5 minutes

1 Spend the next minute just studying these words. Think about what they mean to you.

Tree	Co-ordinate	Connection
Stem	Cerebellum	Fornix
Heart	Satellite	Ghost
Medulla	Thalamus	Amygdala
Feeding	Control	Elephant
Pons	Hypothalamus	Hippocampus
Movement	Reptile	Professor X
Midbrain	Limbic	Cortex

2 Cover the words above. Look at the list of words below and identify any words you have just studied.

Fish	Pons	Medulla
Cortex	Cerebellum	Amygdala
Movement	Thalamus	Limbic
Midbrain	Reptile	Hippocampus
Fornix	Ship	Love
Dinosaur	Pirate	Hypothalamus
Cerebellum	Awesome	Remember

This is one example of explicit memory where you have made a conscious effort to recall.

IMPLICIT (NON-CONSCIOUS) MEMORY

Implicit memory covers several different types of memory that are all considered non-conscious, i.e. you are not making a conscious effort to recall the information, experience or skill.

Try it now: Fill in the blank

Time limit: 2 minutes

Take a few deep breaths and clear your mind. As you breathe slowly count down from 10 to 1.

As you look at the following stubs of words, without thinking about it say the first word that comes to mind. Do this at speed. If nothing comes straight away, move on and come back to it. Write each word you come up with down on a piece of paper.

For   _____
Lim   _____
Po   _____
Mid   _____
Cer   _____
Amy   _____
Hip   _____
Tha   _____
Cor   _____
Med   _____
Hyp   _____
Ele   _____

Although slightly contrived in this situation, since you have previously been primed with potential words for the above stems (Ele – Elephant, etc.), there is a higher probability that this will be one of the words that come to mind. This is called the priming effect.

Whereas explicit memory is conscious recall, implicit memories are related to non-conscious recall. An example of explicit memory would be trying to remember a list of words you have previously seen; an example of implicit memory is knowing how to drive your car, dance or play a sport.

SHORT-TERM MEMORY

In order to keep something in short-term memory, you need to rehearse it in your mind, a new PIN number, for example. With repetition you will be able to transfer that number to long-term memory. Pure short-term memory tends to involve things you don't have some knowledge of (e.g. a phone number). In most cases you will be performing a task that involves manipulating information in your short-term memory while reflecting on information in your long-term memory. This mix is generally known as working memory, 'as short-term memory merges with longer-term memory and experience' (*The Brain: A Neuroscience Primer*, Richard F. Thompson, 1993).

Try it now: Number test...

Time limit: 30 seconds

Remember this number:

5 7 4 0 3 9 1 8 6 6 7 2 9 8 5 1 1 4 0 5

Write down as many of the digits as you can remember in sequence.

Time limit: 10 seconds

Remember this car registration:

BD02 GYU

Unless you are already versed in some form of memory techniques you will probably say this number over and over again as previously mentioned, trying to keep it in your mind through rehearsal. If you happen to get distracted while trying to memorize or recall, it will be hard to keep it in your mind. Most will be able to remember seven numbers, plus or minus two, and without rehearsal short-term memory will last a short amount of time.

In *The Brain: A Neuroscience Primer*, Thompson refers to case studies where people were prevented from rehearsal by counting backwards from 10. The length of time a short-term memory took to decay without rehearsal was about 10 seconds.

Remember this

You could think of short-term memory as one of those aquadoodle mats with water pens. If you haven't seen one, it is basically a drawing mat for kids. You fill a special pen with water and as you draw on the mat the water from the pen makes a colour come through. Like short-term memory whatever you draw fades away unless you keep on going over it. Although an aquadoodle mat may last longer than your short-term memory, it's a nice image to remember how it works.

LONG-TERM MEMORY

Long-term memory is used to cover many types of memory and there are several ways to classify this. We will take a broad view and look at it from the perspective of declarative (explicit) and non-declarative (implicit).

▶ Declarative – knowing that/what (explicit)

Declarative memory and explicit memory are sometimes used interchangeably. Declarative memory includes 'knowing that Shakespeare wrote *Hamlet*', 'knowing what you had for breakfast yesterday' or 'knowing what ingredients make up pancakes'.

Declarative memory is understood fairly well. In 1953 a patient referred to as H.M. had part of his brain removed that included an area of the brain called the hippocampus due to suffering from severe epilepsy. After having surgery, he was still able to remember events and facts from his past. He also still had the ability to remember a string of digits up to the point where he was interrupted. He could also form new implicit memories by being able to perform tasks that were taught to him. However, he could not remember learning to do so. The fact that he could not create new declarative memories led scientists to believe that the hippocampus played an essential role in forming these types of long-term memories. We can break declarative memory into episodic and semantic.

Episodic memory

Try it now: Where have you been?

Time limit: 1 minute

Answer the following questions and write down some key words that capture your answers:

- What was one of your favourite holidays?
- What was the last film you went to see?
- What did you have for breakfast yesterday?

Episodic memory relates to experiences or events that are time-tagged and include spatial information.

Semantic memory

Try it now: What do you know?
Time limit: 1 minute

Answer the following questions and write down your answers
* What is the name of the author of the Harry Potter books?
* What is your partner's or family member's birthday?
* What does mnemonic mean?

Semantic memory is about your knowledge of facts. This could be the elements of the periodic table or knowing that *karova* is Russian for 'cow'. One of the differences between episodic and semantic memory is that semantic memory is not time-tagged to a specific event: you will know that Rome is the capital of Italy but unless you have been there you will probably not have an experience linked to that.

Case study: Believe in the power of memory

Beth was studying Acupuncture and Hermione wanted some general improvements to her memory. Shortly after the workshop I received a letter from each of them. Beth talked about how she had previously failed an acupuncture exam a number of times and after attending the memory workshop she had managed to pass with 100%. This sounded great and started to change my own beliefs about the real world value of learning how to use your memory.

The second letter from Hermione was even more revealing as it talked about a major increase in confidence, how it had changed her life and she now felt she could study and do anything she wanted. Reading it I remember thinking, 'But these are just a bunch of tricks', however as I read on, it made sense that having the ability to remember anything if you applied yourself could have a positive effect on a person's belief system.

Living with a belief that your memory works well when you take on a different way of thinking, is fairly significant. Hermione had an 'experience', a new set of memories that changed how she thought about herself and would potentially affect future decisions about what she may choose to do.

▶ Non-declarative – knowing how (implicit)

Non-declarative is a label grouping various different types of non-conscious memory including:

- ▶ **Procedural** – Knowing how to dance or drive a car or play a sport (motor skills).

- ▶ **Priming** – 'A stimulus influences the response to another stimulus.' There are several examples of implicit memory, we will delve deeper into priming in the next chapter. One example of implicit memory is the test you completed where you received the information (in this case certain words) prior to seeing a stem of those words that resulted in you non-consciously recalling some or all of them.

- ▶ **Conditioning** of responses – e.g. Pavlov's dogs, where they were conditioned to salivate when they heard a bell ring.

Case study: Swim like a dolphin

Emi (CEO of Brainient, an advertising startup) was looking to improve his memory for statistics, presentations and to gain a competitive edge.

In one coaching session the subject of triathlons came up. It turned out that he was having a challenge with the swimming part of the event; he was a good swimmer and understood all of the mechanics, however he needed to get to the point where he could do 25 lengths and he was only doing about seven. Physically he knew he should be able to do more however he was getting caught up in the mechanics.

At first it may not seem that relevant that improving one of the various memory types could help you go from seven to 25 laps. In the session I talked about the idea of implicit learning (Masters, 1992). Implicit learning occurs where the learner is given no explicit verbal instruction, yet still acquires the skills to perform. When working with someone on implicit learning you can offer various metaphors that help reduce 'over thinking' or paralysis by analysis, which was what seemed to be happening with Emi.

Through a series of questions, he came up with a visual metaphor for how he wanted to swim - he was a dolphin! The next day I received a text saying 'I'm a dolphin'; he had just swam the 25 lengths! He didn't suddenly gain more stamina in this 24-hour period, this metaphor was rapidly teaching his body how it was supposed to feel and act thereby removing over analysis and allowing him to go with the flow.

WORKING MEMORY

Bryden (2007) refers to Baddeley (2001) on working memory as a type of memory used to hold information for short periods of time while it is being manipulated. This also encompasses the idea of short-term memory. The picture of working memory involves a central executive that manipulates the information and three storage components:

▶ the phonological loop (subvocal rehearsal)

▶ visuospatial sketchpad (visual and spatial information)

▶ the episodic buffer (information retrieved from long-term episodic memory).

Working memory is essential in evaluating and making decisions.

Try it now: A working memory story
Time limit: 3 minutes

To help remember this model of memory you might imagine yourself as an executive in a large office. To your left is a phonogram. You turn it on and it starts playing the same words over and over again. In front of you is a large canvas with a map of your home town. You paint pictures on different spaces. To your right there is a large HD TV with DVDs that capture episodes from your life. As the executive, you can use these three resources to work with and store new information.

Read this through two more times, letting the images come to mind.

Close your eyes and recite the main points.

Now write down Baddeley's model of working memory.

This is a small taster of creative memorization.

Making connections

Key idea: Building blocks

The building blocks of who we are were apparently discovered by accident after a section of brain was knocked into a petri dish with silver nitrate. It lay there for two weeks before it was found by Camillo Golgi, who with the aid of a microscope was able to identify what is referred to as the neuron. The neuron is the basic information-processing unit, making possible our understanding, memories and behaviours (Diamond, Scheibel, Elson, 1985).

Case study: Brain soup

You may have heard that there are 100 billion neurons in the brain? In actual fact there are around 86 billion. In Dr Suzana Herculano-Houzel's Ted Talk 'What is so special about the human brain?', she describes how they discovered this 86 billion number (Azevedo et al., 2009), by essentially creating a brain soup through a process of dissolving the cell membrane of cells into a homogenous mixture, differentiating neurons from glia, which allows counting of the neurons.

To make it easy to remember this key number, simply imagine that there is a brain soup which you ate (8) with a stick (6). Not very nice, I know but hard to forget.

These 86 billion interconnected neurons make up what we refer to as the structures of the brain. A single neuron can have between 5,000 and 10,000 connections, a potential quadrillion neuronal connections (Sprenger, 1999). This image gives a clue to the vast potential of the human brain.

To picture a neuron in its basic form, you can break it down to the cell body (soma), the tree-like branches (dendrites) sprawling away from the soma in search of incoming information from other neurons, and the longer trunk (axon) looking for other neurons to communicate with and send signals to.

As you look at a neuron, you will see there are many dendrites and only one axon. Signals are sent through the axon and are received by the dendrites. Signals can also be received by dendritic spines (the small spines on the dendrite), axon to soma, axon to axon, dendrite to dendrite and soma to soma (Diamond, Scheibel, Elson, 1985).

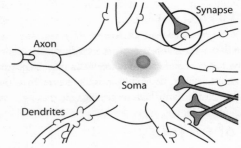

Figure 1.1 A neuron.

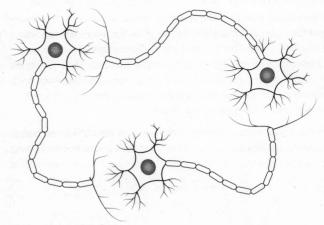

Figure 1.2 A neuronal network.

The purpose of the neuron is to transmit information to other cells. The neuron communicates with other neurons through chemicals reacting and producing electrical signals. As these 'signals' are passed on, the neurons create networks. In real life these networks represent how we perceive the world around us: a particular set of neuronal networks will fire when we try to remember the name of the person standing in front of us; neuronal networks will be constantly firing as you read this book. The amazing thing about the brain is that neuronal networks can change; a particular neuronal network that fires every time you get up to talk in front of people, making you nervous, can be interrupted and changed. If you change the network, you change the behaviour.

As the axon splits into smaller fibres, they end at the axon terminal. When a fibre makes a connection with another cell, it is called a synapse. Between the axon terminal and another neuron or its dendrite is what is called the synaptic cleft (a small gap). In order for a signal to cross over the gap, it needs help from a neurotransmitter, thus the signal can continue on. These signals are constantly firing across the brain.

The art of memory

Memory techniques have been with us since the ancient Greeks over 2,000 years ago. In Frances Yates's non-fiction book *The Art of Memory*, she tells the fascinating story of memory techniques throughout the ages, beginning with Simonides of Ceos who, after giving a poem in honour of his host, a Thessalian named Scopas, was given a message that two men were waiting for him outside. Upon leaving the banquet hall, he found there was no one there. At that moment the roof collapsed and killed everyone inside.

As the bodies were indistinguishable in the rubble, relatives who came to identify them could not recognize them. However, Simonides remembered where everyone had sat by the fact that each person was at a particular place or location and was able to guide their family to them. It was from this experience and the realization that his memory of the guests was connected to the place where they had sat that gave him the reputation as the inventor of the art of memory. The techniques that grew from this point were passed down through the ages from the Romans to European tradition, going on to give particular focus to Giordano Bruno and his works on memory.

Techniques that allow for the storage of a huge range of information are perhaps even more relevant today, in a world where information comes at us from every angle and a multitude of sources. Having been passed down through the ages, in current times these techniques are mostly recognizable through memory experts but are rarely thought of as something which could help children at school or in a business context.

As we move forward, you will recognize that there are many opportunities where you can utilize some of these age-old traditions in a modern way.

While this chapter has focused on types of memory, neurons and inside the brain, it has also been an opportunity to prime yourself with some basic creative memorization concepts. Depending on how actively you participated, you will potentially remember the story about working memory and the story about the brain. Even if you don't, some ideas will have set seed and will grow to support ways of thinking in subsequent sections of the book.

Focus points

* Identify how good your memory is on a scale of 1–10 and how good you would like it to be (you will reference this at the end of the book).
* Explicit memory is conscious (remembering the capital of Ireland or the last movie you watched); implicit memory is non-conscious (riding a bike).
* Priming is when one stimulus influences the response of another stimulus, as in the implicit memory test: what word comes to mind when you see, Ele_____. If you thought of a big creature with a trunk, it's because you were primed for this earlier in the chapter.
* Working memory allows you to manipulate information within your short-term memory and work with information in long-term memory; it enables you to evaluate and make decisions.
* Declarative (explicit) memory is about knowledge (semantic) and experience (episodic). Non-declarative (implicit) memory is about learned skills such as driving a car (procedural) or buying a particular cereal from the supermarket because you have seen it that morning in an advertisement (primed).
* The information-processing units of your brain are the neurons: they make you who you are, allowing you to understand, remember and act. There are around 86 billion neurons, each with a possible 5,000–10,000 connections.
* Signals are passed between neurons, sent via the axon and received by dendrites (signals can also be received by dendritic spines, soma and axon).
* Simonides of Ceos was renowned as the inventor of the art of memory.
* There are huge opportunities to use our understanding of types of memory and the art of memory in our modern lives.

Next steps

By understanding *why* you want to improve your memory, *what* it can do for you and the various memory *types*, you start to understand the positive impact of a better memory. Imagine being able to remember anything, influence your own behaviours and master skills in any area of your life?

2

The learning cycle: Take control of your memory

In this chapter you will learn:

► *the learning cycle and how you can use it*
► *using reflection to create understanding and memory*
► *the benefits of questioning your learning*
► *how to complete the loop through testing your thoughts and ideas*
► *how to prime your senses.*

In James E. Zull's book *The Art of Changing the Brain*, he explores and suggests a method for teaching that utilizes research into experiential learning by David Kolb. Zull uses his knowledge of biology and experience as a teacher to demonstrate the usefulness and application of the learning cycle and how it maps to the way our brain works, how we learn and how it can be used as a model for teachers to improve learning for their students.

The subject itself is extensive, and the purpose of this chapter is to explore the learning cycle model from a high level in order to identify how it can be used to frame techniques in later chapters.

Key idea: The learning cycle

At the most basic level, the learning cycle works on the premise that we receive experiences through our senses, we integrate those experiences into our thinking by reflecting on what we know, associating with our memories and ideas, questioning and abstracting our own ideas, then complete the cycle by taking some form of action to test what we have learned.

Sense → integrate → act

The learning cycle is not set in stone. Numerous cycles can happen simultaneously. This is our natural process of learning. Different people will play with the learning cycle in different ways. Some might come up with great ideas and follow through on them yet claim to have a poor memory. Others will have the ability to remember lots of facts but not really comprehend and be able to put what they remember into action. Each of these types will be focusing their efforts more on one area of the learning cycle than another.

Remember this

Understanding and being aware of the learning cycle can give us the opportunity to be more effective in how we learn and more importantly how we use what we learn.

Try it now: Explore the learning cycle
Time limit: 5 minutes

Whether we are aware of it or not, we are continuously learning. Throughout our lives, some of those lessons will have a positive effect and some a negative effect. Below is an illustration of the 'idea' of the learning cycle.

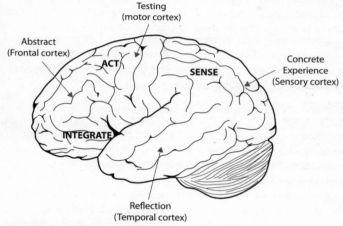

Figure 2.1 The learning cycle.

Complete the following actions:
* Study the learning cycle diagram.
* Think about what it reminds you of: what does it mean to you, what images or words does it spark off in your mind?
* Think about how you might utilize this cycle to comprehend and remember something of importance to you.
* Now write down your thoughts, or draw a picture, and either explain to a friend what you think it means or explain it out loud to yourself.

By running through the above four steps you have just gone through the learning cycle. As previously mentioned, we are constantly running a number of cycles, taking in new sensory information, reflecting on what it means, abstracting our own ideas, reflecting on those, taking some kind of action to test them out, receiving more sensory information and so on.

Case study: Different strokes

Are you a big picture thinker or do you like to get into the details? A number of years ago while working with two clients (brother and sister), it was interesting to observe how opposite they were in the way they approached learning, what they believed they were good at and where they had challenges.

The brother had an amazing ability to remember and understand details, while the sister was instinctively good at seeing component parts to problems and was a big picture and strategic thinker. However they both initially seemed to lack what the other possessed.

The obstacle was making them aware of how they were each using the learning cycle and by making small shifts in their thinking they could each grow in areas in which the other excelled.

For the sister this meant being able to have techniques to store, understand and recall details at the appropriate time. This involved directing her focus to reflect on what she already knew thereby making stronger connections with new information. A specific example was to ask herself 'What does this new information mean to me?'; by asking this question her brain would make new connections when faced with a fact that didn't immediately make sense and then the addition of creative memorization would make it stick.

For the brother, the suggestion was to spend more time abstracting his own thoughts and find ways to see the big picture so he could build relationships with all of the various details in his mind. Strategies included getting clearer on outcomes, visual note-taking and mind mapping.

With these strategies they were able to make transformations in how they approached learning and develop their expertise.

Let us look at each section of the learning cycle in more detail.

CONCRETE EXPERIENCE (SENSE)
We are constantly experiencing a multitude of sensory information from the outside world. That information is

directed to the area of the brain that deals with sensory information. Zull refers to this as the sensory cortex, a term used to group various regions of the cerebral cortex that deal with touch, taste, vision, sound and smell. This variety of sensory input represents your concrete experience.

REFLECTIVE OBSERVATION (INTEGRATE)
Reflection happens in the temporal integrative cortex. Our reflective skills allow us to integrate the concrete experience we have received via our senses into something tangible that has meaning.

Long-term explicit memories are formed in this region, in which the hippocampus plays a major role. The left hemisphere allows us to comprehend the detail of language and the right hemisphere the meaning with regard to how things are being said, intonation and intention. We will find ourselves drifting off in a daydream state, finding connections to related images.

This reflective process may respond with images and memories similar to the new incoming information. When we read that there are 86 billion brain cells in the brain, while reflecting on this we remember brain soup, which you ate (8) with a stick (6).

ABSTRACT HYPOTHESIS (INTEGRATE)
Our front integrative cortex allows us to build on what we know, create new connections, explore possibilities, judge whether it makes sense based on what we know, use our working memory to manipulate the information, question our back integrative cortex for more information and bring all this back and make evaluations based on our experience.

If the concrete information has not made any sense to us, it can work with the back integrative cortex, questioning for possible meaning. It can create new images and 'what if' scenarios, effectively helping to construct possible new memories.

In short, it is the director of your brain, allowing us to take ownership of the information, make decisions about it and prime us for action: the Steven Spielberg of your mind – creating, editing, questioning and producing something that can be acted upon.

ACTIVE TESTING (ACT)

If the front integrative cortex is the director, the pre-motor and motor cortex are the actors, taking action in the form of voluntary movement and speech. Testing out ideas in order to receive more sensory information. This action may come in the form of speaking, rehearsing, building, writing or moving.

Try it now: Using the learning cycle

Time limit: 5 minutes

* Sensory input: How would you use this model to help remember that the capital city of Madagascar is Antananarivo?
* Reflection: What memories, images and understandings do you have about Madagascar and Antananarivo? What comes to mind?
* Abstraction: How might you make this information more memorable? What do you need to know?
* Action: Find out what you need to know. Draw a picture to represent the information, write the words or make them out of clay and say them aloud. Explain how you did this to a friend; ask how they might do it.

It is likely that you will jump around and do some of these things out of sequence, perhaps run the cycle a number of times.

Remember this

When I first started using memory techniques back in the early 1990s, it seemed clear to me that to truly understand, you have to experience, and to remember that experience, it has to have meaning and a purpose for you. If you are a programmer, there is no use in just understanding syntax, you need to physically build applications to fully appreciate the craftsmanship involved. If you learn a language, you have to go and put it into practice for it to become implicitly useful. As the saying goes, 'If you don't use it, you lose it.' As clichéd as this is, it stands true, even more so when we understand that our brain's neuronal networks get stronger the more they fire off and, if they stop firing, those connections can stop working.

Emotion and motivation

> ## Key idea: Emotion
> Joining the learning cycle together is emotion, the area in the limbic cortex that lets us experience pain and pleasure. Emotions are our motivators. They can prime us and direct our attention; they can intensify our memories and add meaning to them.

You instinctively know that if you are interested in something, you are more likely to remember it; likewise if you are afraid of something or you know that something will be a painful experience, you will definitely remember this in order to avoid it.

You could use this knowledge to prime yourself for key information within a book, presentation or seminar. Your reticular activation system (reticular formation), located within your brain stem, is permanently turned on – it directs your attention to anything that is of importance to you. You may have had the experience when you have bought a new computer. You loved it, it gave you loads of pleasure, until now you haven't noticed anyone with one, you thought you were the first to get one – but now suddenly 'everyone' has one. Your senses have been primed!

> ## Case study: The priming effect
> In Daniel Kahneman's book, *Thinking Fast and Slow* he talks about the priming effect, referring to a number of studies psychologists ran in the 1980s and 90s. These include how 'exposure to a word causes immediate and measureable changes in the ease with which many related words can be evoked'.
>
> An example of this would be if you had recently heard the word EAT, or had seen images of hot, tasty food with chunks of bread and butter and when asked to fill in the blank to what would you put here; SO...P, it would most likely be SOUP. On the other hand, if you had seen the word WASH or had been watching a film about a detective who finds a murdered body. When asked to fill in the blank you would most likely complete it as SOAP.

Priming in your life

You have already experienced priming in the first chapter where you were presented with a set of stub words and then asked to complete them (e.g. *ele*........ would be completed as *elephant*).

Think about other types of priming in your own life. Have you ever:

► watched a scary film late at night and were more aware of creaking and noises in your house as you lay there in bed?

► bought a new item of clothing and started to notice more people wearing the same as you?

► been in an environment, which felt creative and perhaps the décor was had lots of greens or blues?

Remember this

Priming has much more of an impact in your life than this though, once you understand how it influences your decisions and actions, you can use it to take more control of how you can learn more effectively.

Try this now: Priming your senses for learning
Time limit: 3 minutes

Do you want to learn how to be more focused and attentive when reading books, listening to presentations, studying or catching someone's name?

✻ **Books**: Ask yourself this question to prime yourself to remember information within a book. What will this book give me? What level of detail do I need to understand? What could surprise me about this book?

✻ **Presentations**: Think about a great presentation you have been to in the past

✻ **Studying**: Think about some past learning successes

✻ **Names**: What is interesting about this person?

Try it now: How priming can make you miss things

Time limit: 1 minute

- Take a moment to look around the room.
- Try to remember everything you see that is shaped like a SQUARE.
- Do this now before reading on...
- Now keep looking at this book – DO NOT LOOK AWAY!
- With your EYES CLOSED say out loud everything in the room that is shaped like a circle.
- What have you learned from this?

Framing your learning

The learning cycle is a great way of 'framing' how we think about learning that creates understanding and is memorable. It makes sure that when working with new information, you touch on every stage.

In the upcoming chapters we will build on the knowledge of our model of how memory works and the learning cycle and show how you can utilize specific techniques and a way of thinking that will rapidly increase your effectiveness in how to remember and deliver value from your actions.

We will be exploring how you can become more receptive to sensory information. How can you create the optimum environment both externally and internally for the sensory information you receive? You will learn techniques to improve reflection and abstraction that will help with memory and understanding, all with a view to what action can be taken.

Key idea: Living the learning cycle

You might want to think of the rest of this book as 'living' the learning cycle. As you are exposed to some new ideas or information, be encouraged to reflect on your own experiences, explore and take ownership of where this fits in with your own life, become an active participant by putting what you learn into practice.

Focus points

* Use the basis of the learning cycle, Sense → Integrate → Act to frame all your learning.
* You have a concrete experience through a multitude of sensory inputs.
* Reflective observation relates sensory input to things you already know in a search for understanding and meaning.
* Use abstract hypothesis to deeply integrate new information through questioning and exploring possibilities.
* Put what you have learned into practice through active testing and receive feedback in the form of more sensory input allowing you to learn and grow.
* Emotion is the motivator: get curious and look for how new information will help you achieve your purpose and give you pleasure and avoid pain.
* Prime yourself before reading a book or listening to a presentation by thinking about what might be important to you.
* Become an active participant in your learning; use everything you learn in some way.

Next steps

Set yourself up to create the best learning experiences. Get clear on how 'you' go through the learning cycle, notice where priming crops up in your life and look for opportunities to prime yourself to achieve the outcomes you want.

Part Two

A new way of thinking

'Imagination is everything. It is the preview of life's coming attractions.'

Albert Einstein

3

Creative memorization: Unleash your true memory potential

In this chapter you will learn:

- ▶ *the process for creative memorization*
- ▶ *becoming present and living in the moment*
- ▶ *how to develop the four core skills*
- ▶ *how to make information more memorable*
- ▶ *how to put creative memorization into practice.*

Memory and creativity

Key idea: Memorization

At the heart of memorization are sets of skills that allow us to remember vast amounts of information, store it in long-term memory and recall it at any time with minimal revision. You can think of this set of skills as creative memorization. Once mastered, it is possible to memorize an entire book, remember the names of 50 people in a room or details of an hour-long presentation.

At the heart of creative memorization are four core skills:

► **Flow** – the ability to become completely present 'in the moment' and enter into a focused state of mind, free from tension, distractions or inhibitions

► **Imagination** – to create life-like experiences using all of your senses and emotion

► **Association** – to find creative ways of connecting, questioning and analysing

► **Meaning** – understand what something means to you using metaphor, simile or analogy, thereby increasing comprehension

The good news is you already possess the skills you need to memorize anything you put your mind to; in fact, as a child you probably spent most of your time strengthening them. However, through lack of use some may have diminished over time. With creative memorization the difference between a person's ability to remember or forget is all about approach and the intensity with which these skills are applied.

Remember this

In practice you want to remember that Burkina Faso's capital is Ouagadougou. Using creative memorization you see a BARKING dog with a mean FACE (Barkin' Face, Burkina Faso) but he is a good WAGGY

DOGGY (Waggy Doggy, Ouagadougou). By repeating the 'real words' aloud and 'seeing' the image simultaneously, you create a strong connection between the image and the information. You now know that Ouagadougou is the capital of Burkina Faso.

Try it now: Benchmark your core skills
Time limit: 5 minutes

Take a moment to write down the answers to the following questions:
* What are the things you currently do to relax and release tension?
* How do you achieve a concentrated and focused state of mind?
* Think of a time when you had to be imaginative. Where were you, what were you doing, what challenges did you have and what was the outcome?
* How good are you at making connections, solving problems and identifying patterns? When have you done this and what were the results?
* On a scale of 1–10 (10 being excellent), how good would you say you were at each one of these core skills?
* On a piece of A4 paper write down each of the four core skills or draw a picture which represents them. Next to each one write down the number you gave for the level you are currently at. Stick this up where it will be visible. We will use this to measure your improvement over the course of the book.

Memory techniques have been around for over 2,000 years and have been reinvented many times. The essence of creative memorization is the ability to use our imagination and association to construct vivid memories that can be stored and easily recalled.

Try it now: Test your association skills
Time limit: 5 minutes

Read the following ten words and say aloud the first word you associate with each one, then write it down. It is important not to 'think' too hard or edit what is in your mind even if you think it is ridiculous – for Ricky Gervais you might say 'funny', 'loud' or 'the office'. The associations you come up with will be personal to you.

* Ricky Gervais
* Dumbo
* Chaplin
* Nemo
* Ugly
* Fight
* Caboose
* French
* Smoke
* Karova

For every word in this list (whether you are aware of it or not) you will have an image sparked off by an association you have with it. In some cases, as with Nemo, it may be because you have watched the film *Finding Nemo*, so you say the word 'fish', this is a natural association. With a word like *karova*, unless you know that it is Russian for 'cow', your image may have been 'a car' because the first part of the word sounds like 'car ', 'Car – rova' or a bottle of 'Corona'. Even though you don't know what it means, your brain will go searching for a connection and bring something back. Perhaps you read one of these words and simply told yourself that you didn't know what it means, in which case you may have had a brief image of the word itself and then your brain ceased looking for an association.

Remember this

Your brain will pay close attention to what you say. Have you ever had the experience of meeting someone who you haven't seen for a long time, you recognize their face, know that you knew them, perhaps even really well, but you just can't remember the name, then a couple of days or weeks later their name pops into your mind? The reason behind this is that you asked a question with the expectation of getting an answer and so your brain goes off in search of one. If, on the other hand, you told yourself 'I can't remember' or 'I don't know it', your brain will stop looking for those connections.

The creative state of mind

Konstantin Stanislavsky, renowned for the Stanislavsky acting technique, referred to the creative state of mind as 'the artistic condition that frees the body of tension and energizes the creative faculties' (from Mel Gordon's *The Stanislavsky Technique*).

THE STANISLAVSKY TECHNIQUE

The Stanislavsky technique contains a set of exercises to improve relaxation, concentration and imagination, which culminate in the ability to enter into what Stanislavsky referred to as the 'creative state of mind'. In Mel Gordon's workbook for actors, *The Stanislavsky Technique*, he pulls together techniques used throughout Stanislavsky's life.

▶ Konstantin Stanislavsky

In 1912 Konstantin Stanislavsky (originally, Konstantin Sergeyevich Alexeyev) opened the Moscow Art Theatre's first studio, condensing years of work into a set of specific techniques, known as the Stanislavsky techniques. Two of his greatest students, Yevgeny Vakhtangov and Michael Chekhov, went on to create variations of his work, influencing actors around the globe for years to come. In the USA, Lee Strasberg created 'The Method', a system derived from Stanislavsky's techniques which is now mostly known through actors such as Dustin Hoffman, Robert De Niro, Marilyn Monroe, James Dean and Paul Newman to name but a few.

There are and always have been differences of opinion as to the value of Stanislavsky's techniques to innately talented actors. An example of this might be the infamous conversation between Dustin Hoffman (a 'method' actor) and Laurence Olivier on the set of the film *Marathon Man* (1976), where Hoffman had apparently been running around the block in preparation for a scene in which he was out of breath. When Olivier, bemused by this behaviour, asked what he was doing, Hoffman questioned how else could he prepare for the scene. To which Olivier retorted, 'Try acting, dear boy.' Whether this is true or not, in acting circles it is a story which is retold when debate breaks out about the Stanislavsky technique or 'The Method'.

Many of these techniques provide a useful framework when it comes to improving the core skills required in creative memorization.

Remember this

The techniques laid down by Stanislavsky provide numerous ways in which to enter the creative state of mind. However you access it, this state is exactly the place you need to be when you wish to comprehend, store, retain and recall information. It is no coincidence that the majority of competent actors have the ability to memorize numerous plays word for word and recite monologues from them years later. Although actors may not be aware of it, they are using very similar creative memorization skills employed by memory champions to remember over 2,000 digits in an hour. Other techniques from Stanislavsky to do with objectives, actions, justification and units provide an excellent framework when memorizing more advanced information such as books, law, speeches and presentations.

Core skills

FLOW

There are many ways of achieving states of relaxation and becoming 'present': regular meditation or exercises such as tai chi, yoga, qigong and pilates are excellent in releasing tension, energizing and creating an awareness of your body. For creative memorization the ideal state is to be relaxed, energized and free from tension. This state doesn't have to be still, you can just as easily be in this state of flow when you are playing tennis, dancing or giving a presentation.

Case study: Mindfulness training

In 2013 research by Michael D Mrazek (Mrazek et al., 2013), at Santa Barbara University in California, took 48 students and placed half of them on a nutrition course and the other half on a mindfulness training course (each for two weeks). Their objectives were to reduce mind-wandering and improve cognitive performance.

The results demonstrated that mindfulness training reduced mind-wandering in participants who were normally prone to distraction. It also improved GRE reading comprehension and working memory capacity.

The research stated: 'Our results suggest that cultivating mindfulness is an effective and efficient technique for improving cognitive function, with wide-reaching consequences.'

Try it now: Three-minute breathing space

You can do this anytime you have a break – perhaps if you have popped out for walk in your lunch break – your eyes don't need to be closed.

* **Check**: Spend one minute becoming aware of what is happening in your body Thoughts Feelings
* **Breathe**: Spend one minute breathing into any area of tension, letting go of thoughts and feelings
* **Expand**: Spend one minute expanding your awareness back into your body Thoughts Feelings

Key idea: Mindfulness for flow

Practising mindfulness techniques is an excellent strategy for entering into the state of flow, allowing you to more readily and effortlessly let yourself be fully in the moment. When this happens consistently you may well discover that you have enhanced productivity, reduced stress and are naturally building momentum towards your goals.

With less stress you will naturally have a superior memory than when you are anxious about what could be. You may also notice that your energy increases and you can more easily channel it towards your various activities, projects or passions without feeling distracted.

Below is a mindmap from Martha Langley's 'The Mindfulness Workbook' and a five-step process to remember it. During a live webinar I shared with a group how I used priming, previewing, speed reading, probing and performing to remember this book in 3-4 hours

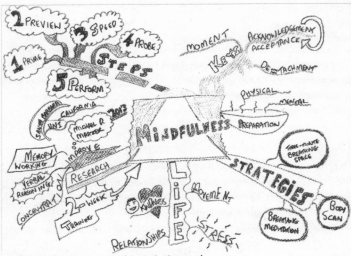

(Hand-drawn mind map by Mark Channon)

There are many ways that you can practise entering into the moment; each of the following activities for Focus, Imagination and Association can all help you practise being in the here and now.

Try it now: Achieve energy and relaxation

Time limit: 10 minutes

* Try this deep diaphragmatic breathing exercise that will relax, focus and energize your body. Breathe at this ratio – in for 1 hold for 4 out for 2 – so you may breathe in for 8, hold for 32 out for 16. Repeat this 10 times. Practise this three times a day to relax and increase energy (from *Personal Power*, Tony Robbins).

* Sit on a chair, get yourself into a comfortable position and just be aware of your body pressing against the chair. While breathing deeply pay attention to each part of your body in turn, starting with your feet and working through your knees, thighs, all the way up to the top of your

head. As you work your way up, notice how much tension there is. Each time you notice some tension, take a breath and breathe out to release it.

✳ Clench the fist of your right hand, breathe in and as you breathe out let go of all tension. Repeat this with your left fist, then feel the tension releasing from your entire body.

✳ Pick up an object and notice how much energy is needed. Put it down. Try it again and this time use the least amount of energy possible, become aware of which muscles are engaging, put the object down and release all tension from your muscles. Repeat this exercise with different objects (from *The Stanislavsky Technique*, Mel Gordon).

FOCUS

Relaxation and concentration are closely connected. Together they create a state of focus ideal for memorization. With practice you can train yourself to a level where you can block out all distractions.

Try it now: Concentration and focus

Time limit: 10 minutes

✳ Focus on a spot on the wall while picking up the sounds of everything around you. While focusing on this spot, identify each sound before moving on to the next one. See how many sounds you can identify and try to judge where they are coming from.

✳ Turn on the TV, then the radio, and at the same time have someone try to engage you in conversation while you perform a task that requires concentration. This might be reading a book, writing some emails or solving a problem.

✳ Begin several activities: look at magazine pictures, listen to music, solve a mathematical problem, play a game, check your email, make a phone call. Move quickly from one activity to another. In each activity, concentrate completely on the first before you pass on to the next (from *The Stanislavsky Technique*, Mel Gordon).

✳ Close your eyes and mentally transport yourself to a location of your choice. Walk around that location paying close attention to objects (from *The Stanislavsky Technique*, Mel Gordon).

IMAGINATION

Imagination is the foundation of creative memorization. The ability not just to create vivid images using all of our five senses but to suspend belief about what is and isn't possible, take ourselves into a world of fantasy, excite our curiosity and recapture those childlike moments of inspiration.

By strengthening this skill, it is possible to intensify the memories we create, bring them alive, exaggerate them, give them rhythm and movement and make them instantly memorable, transferring them into long-term memory.

Try it now: Engaging your imagination

Time limit: 10 minutes

* Focus on a simple object, study it, then recreate it in your mind in every detail. Engage each of your five senses.
* Focus on a different object; imagine it sprouting arms, legs and a face. Ask what it wants and listen to what it says. Now close your eyes and recreate the object, notice where you visualize the object in your mind, have a conversation with the object. Try switching between eyes closed and eyes open.
* Imagine a flower growing from a seed in the ground into a full plant. Closing your eyes, follow the process of its growth and development (from *The Stanislavsky Technique*, Mel Gordon).
* Remember a street or path that you walk past daily. Break it into separate sections. Create a story that links each of the sections of the street (from *The Stanislavsky Technique*, Mel Gordon).
* Find resemblances between objects and specific persons. Find resemblances between selected persons and animals. Study them in your mind (from *The Stanislavsky Technique*, Mel Gordon).

AFFECTIVE MEMORY

A key skill in the Stanislavsky technique was the ability to recreate feelings and emotions; while this is obviously useful for an actor, it is also a skill that can greatly intensify a memory. Stanislavsky referred to this as 'affective memory' and it can be broken down into two parts: sense memory, which allows you to create sensations, and emotional recall, which allows you to create emotion.

Remember this

In creative memorization the skill of not just seeing the image in your mind but feeling, tasting, hearing and smelling it, as well as incorporating emotions such as joy, humour, tragedy, fear or arousal, allows you to go much further than simply turning information into pictures: it translates potentially dry or complex information into memorable experiences.

Try it now: Develop your sense memory (creating concrete experience)

Time limit: 10 minutes

✻ Make a cup of tea, paying close attention to every movement and sense. As you drink it, notice the various sensations in your body. Now create another cup of tea using only your imagination, recreate every feeling in detail – pay attention to all five senses.

✻ Imagine you are waiting for a bus in the rain, you don't have a jacket and it's cold. Close your eyes and recreate what it feels like – make it real and engage each one of your senses. Now imagine someone else is at the bus stop: how do they feel?

✻ Light a match. Repeat the activity until you strongly feel every detail of it. Now perform the activity again without the actual matches (from *The Stanislavsky Technique*, Mel Gordon).

✻ Complete the following activities without any real objects: wash your hair, put clothes on, shave, sew with a needle, sharpen a pencil, now sharpen a pencil with a knife. Create a complete and convincing action without worrying about the miming of each activity (from *The Stanislavsky Technique*, Mel Gordon).

Try it now: Develop your emotional recall

Time limit: 10 minutes

✻ Remember all the foods you ate as a child. Describe their flavours and textures. Experience the taste of them and how you felt (from *The Stanislavsky Technique*, Mel Gordon).

* Remember the house or flat where you grew up. Describe it. Imagine you are there now and notice the emotions you feel (from *The Stanislavsky Technique*, Mel Gordon).
* Think back to the first day of school. Now focus on an object, maybe your school bag, notice the smell and how heavy it is. Remember a situation from one of those early days and experience the emotions you had.
* Imagine it is late at night and you are sitting on the sofa when you hear a bang in another room. Experience how that feels. Imagine you can hear creaking floorboards and then the light switches off. Take a moment to analyse the intensity of the emotions you experienced.
* Imagine it's late at night and there is a knock on the door. As you walk to the door you can hear the familiar voices of your friends, you open the door and see two of your friends being held by four large men with balaclavas. Again take a moment to notice the intensity of your sensations.

Choose one sense memory exercise and one emotional recall exercise and this time gauge where you are on a scale of 1–10.

► Practise minimizing and magnifying your senses and emotions along that scale.

► Notice the differences and see how quickly you can change levels of feeling and emotion.

ASSOCIATION

When we think of a past event, we are reminded of details associated with it. We remember Christmas, birthdays and holidays because they have strong associations, they are emotional and have excited our senses.

The events that happen to us affect how we feel, how we act and what we remember. Association is a very powerful tool when it comes to memorizing information. If imagination is the foundation of creative memorization, association is the glue that binds those memories together – imagination and association are intrinsically linked. Throughout our lives we are constantly creating associations; memories, beliefs or feelings we have towards people and things are all formed through various types of associations. The more intense the association, the more memorable it becomes as our neurons form strong synaptic connections.

Association focuses on key left-brain activities such as questioning, analytical thinking and recognizing patterns. In creative memorization this translates into looking for the best way to encode information into images and connect them in a manner that is memorable.

▶ Natural-image and sound-image associations

When it comes to thinking up an image to represent a word or piece of information, there is not always an instant association or at least not one that feels very clear. When there is not a natural association, you will need to create an image that sounds similar to all or part of the keyword; this is known as a sound-image association and is a vital skill to develop if you want to progress to advanced levels of creative memorization.

There are two methods for doing this that with practice become second nature. With both methods the meaning of the word can play an essential part in creating an image for your information.

▶ Natural-image associations – images sparked off by a memory, sense or emotion.

▶ Sound-image associations – images that sound very similar to the information you are memorizing.

Natural-image association

These are all very personal, so I will give you examples of how these words relate to myself; chances are they will have a very different meaning for you.

▶ Awesome – the first image that comes to mind for me is an awesome tidal wave. So I would use tidal wave as my image.

▶ Fearless – a fearless lion or someone you know who was fearless in the past.

▶ Scary – Freddy Kruger, or a similar kind of scary image.

Sound-image association

▶ Madagascar – if you have been here, then you may have an emotional association. If not, we need to look at how the word sounds: a mad – gas – car could represent Madagascar.

▶ Capitulate – the first part of the word is cap, so your image could be a cap. The meaning of capitulate is to surrender or give up. So you could imagine a cap kneeling down with his hands clasped together, surrendering, giving up. This way you remember the word and also what it means.

▶ Accentuate – the first part of this word sounds like axe, so your image could be an axe. Accentuate means to emphasize, highlight, make more noticeable. So you could imagine your axe in a spotlight, emphasizing its tap dancing skills.

As you can probably see, this is also a great way to expand your vocabulary.

▶ Recite the information

An important point to note is that when you look at your mental image you should speak the word out loud; the more obscure the word, the more important this is. By doing this you are creating more mental connections with the image and the sound of the word and helping to lock it in your mind. Within the context of the learning cycle, you are actively testing.

Obviously memorizing like this will seem strange at first, but then again, what new thing we learn doesn't? As I said before, practise something enough and it will eventually become second nature; when it's second nature, it feels the natural thing to do.

Try it now: Natural-image and sound-image association
Time limit: 5 minutes

The easiest way to develop this skill is to practise turning random words into images. The sound-image is a trigger for the real word. Here is an example of how you could use both sound-images and natural associations to make words more memorable. While imagining the following you should be in a relaxed, focused state and engage all of your five senses. It is essential to say the word aloud while visualizing it in your mind:

* Chore – you're dressed like Cinderella doing a chore – say 'chore' aloud (natural)
* Astride – you are astride a horse – say 'astride' aloud (natural)
* Subscript – there is a SUBmarine reading a SCRIPT – say 'subscript' aloud (sound)
* Misjudge – a MISS JUDGE (sound)
* Purified – a purifying filtration unit (natural)
* Braised – a braised bit of beef (natural)
* Semblance – SAME BLINDS (sound)
* Covertly – special ops under a COVER (natural/sound)
* Bravo – clapping, shouting 'Bravo!' (natural)
* Mantel – hanging off the mantel (natural)
* August – Roman Emperor (natural)

▶ The power of questions

Questions are the guiding force for your associations so it is important to ask the right questions in order to receive a good answer. You should also create a feeling of expectation while asking the question. If you expect to get an answer, at some point you will receive feedback. It may not always be the answer you are looking for, but you will get a response. The power of asking questions is essential in your ability not only to create associations but also to recall them.

Try it now: What are your key questions?
Time limit: 5 minutes

Reflect on some of the questions below and ask yourself which ones would be useful to you with regard to creative memorization:

* How can I do this?
* What would happen if?
* What am I missing?
* What's the best way to connect this?

* How can I make this funnier, scarier or sexy?
* How can I intensify this?
* What happens next?
* What shouldn't happen next?
* If I were that object/image, what would I do?
* Where is the best place for this?

Choose or create five key questions you will ask when using creative memorization.

In practice

Creative memorization is exactly what it says: the process of using your creativity to make information more memorable. The pair game is a simple game that allows you to unite the core skills within creative memorization – Relaxation, Concentration, Imagination and Association. The objective of the game is to memorize as many pairs of words as possible.

Try it now: The pair game
Time limit: 5 minutes

* Use the relaxation and concentration technique of your choice; with practice you will be able to go into this focused state almost instantaneously.
* Look at the first pair of words and let an image for each word come into your mind – go for the first natural image that appears. If it doesn't appear straight away, use your questioning skills to figure out what would be a good sound-image.
* Once you have an image for each word, associate them together – for Krypton + Plug, you may imagine Superman wearing a plug made of kryptonite trying to throw it off before he collapses.
* Use your imagination to intensify the images and engage senses. You may imagine that you are Superman and physically act out the scene.
* Finally, repeat the words aloud 3–5 times while focusing on the image – this is essential to associate the words to the image.

Give yourself five minutes to play this game. At the end you will be tested to see how many pairs of words you remember by seeing one of the words and responding with its corresponding pair, e.g. What is the pair word for 'plug'?

krypton + plug

pyramid + camera

laptop + ribbon

speaker + frustration

phone + sing

pencil + trumpet

cola + fast

establish + no

lightning + green

soft + consult

friend + armour

weights + sea

gift + product

radio + Chris

section + blow

Write down the correct word next to its pair:

consult

camera

laptop

section

sing

pencil

cola

krypton

no

lightning

Chris

armour

sea

gift

frustration

The concepts and ideas behind creative memorization are fairly simple; mastering them, however, takes dedication. By immersing yourself in these techniques, the benefits and rewards will become clear as you start to apply them in your everyday life.

Focus points

✳ Creative memorization is the skill to become completely present and use your creative abilities to rapidly increase learning and memory.

✳ Start using the three-minute breathing space and learn more about mindfulness strategies.

✳ Make a note of the level at which you benchmarked your skills so you can compare the results at the end of the book.

✳ Practise some simple relaxation techniques you can use before learning so your body is free from tension; consider an activity such as qigong, tai chi or yoga.

✳ Practise trying to remember something while being distracted, to improve your focus.

✳ Notice everyday objects and recreate them in your mind, involving all of your five senses to strengthen your imagination.

✳ Act out day-to-day activities such as making the tea to develop your sense memory.

✳ Practise remembering events and situations and recall the emotion to intensify the memory.

✳ While practising sense memory and emotional recall, play with the levels of intensity by imagining magnifying the feelings on a scale from 1–10.

✳ Play with turning words into natural-images and sound-images to build your creative memorization skills.

✳ Use the power of questions to guide 'how' you associate information and make it memorable.

Next steps

The skills that you have encountered in this chapter will not only improve your memory, they will set you on the road to becoming less distracted and highly focused.

Spend some time thinking about the different elements of creative memorization: Flow, Imagination, Association and Meaning. Visualize these elements for a moment in a way that has meaning for YOU.

When you think of creative memorization and each of these elements in this way what does it tell you about the way you think? How do they map to you? Now consider some simple ways you can create some space for creative memorization in your daily routines.

If you were to naturally operate in this way what changes would you begin to observe?

4

Reference stories: Making information memorable

In this chapter you will learn:

► *how to create a reference story*
► *being 'selective' when encoding or decoding information*
► *dialling up your stories to make them stick*
► *how to use active daydreaming when you get stumped.*

Encoding

ENCODING AND DECODING

When applying the process of creative memorization, you are effectively encoding, storing and retrieving (decoding) reference stories. Each reference story will act as a 'reference' to the actual information that will presumably benefit you in some way. You may think of a reference story as a container that holds a set of natural-images and/or sound-images: the meaning of these images refers to some real-world information. Therefore a reference story is the tangible artefact you produce when using creative memorization.

When creating reference stories, you have the option to use visual embedding or narratives. The narratives may have context and feel like a micro-story while visual embedding uses a repetitive pattern for associations. The latter is often used by memory athletes to quickly store numbers in competition by visually embedding images from left to right or top to bottom along a pre-ordained journey.

Remember this

Encoding is the process of converting your information into reference stories. Here are the steps you go through when encoding information using creative memorization:

* Identify the information you wish to remember.
* Reflect on your natural-images and/or sound-images.
* Abstract and create your reference story using either a narrative or visual embedding.
* Actively test your story by reciting aloud, writing it down or using it in some way – *important: you must mentally see the images as you say the 'real' information.*

Decoding

Remember this

Decoding is the ability to deconstruct a reference story and convert it back into the information. The following is an example of the steps you go through to decode a reference story:

* You may be asked a question or try to recall the information.
* This will trigger the memory of the reference story.
* Decode the reference story into its component parts and understand its meaning.
* With repetition you will eventually bypass the reference story and just 'know' the information.

Visual embedding

Visual embedding is a simple and consistent approach that you can use when memorizing small chunks of information. You follow the same pattern of connecting images each time, usually from left to right or top to bottom.

Try it now: How to use visual embedding

Time limit: 5 minutes

* Take your main item (in this case the cow).
* You can embed up to three bits of information on to the cow (these items should be smaller).
* The positions you can embed go from top to bottom (head, middle, feet).
* While embedding, use sense memory to experience the connections.
* After embedding zoom back and see the big picture.
* As you look at the image say [image] – [meaning]: [cow] – [karova].
* Repeat 5–20 times at speed.

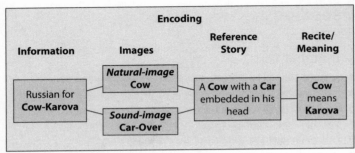

Figure 4.1 Encoding (1).

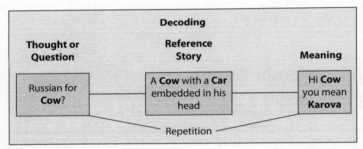

Figure 4.2 Decoding (1).

Narratives

Narratives form a micro-story to connect information together in a sequence; they don't necessarily form any consistent pattern and can therefore be different every time. They often play with the context of the information being memorized. A Cow looking up at the sky sees a Car jumping over the moon. Taking something previously related to the word and changing the context.

Try it now: How to use narratives

Time limit: 5 minutes

Utilizing imagination in your narratives

* Always engage your senses
* Exaggerate your images in some way

* Bring them to life (involve your emotions)

Optional
* Put yourself in the story or imagine you are characters in the story
* Imagine your images in front of you

Associations
* Don't over analyse your associations – anything is possible
* Focus on connecting 2–3 items together at a time
* Connect using a narrative
* Use movement and action to create 'a flow'

Optional
* Act out! If you are in the story while you see the images in front of you, this is a form of actively testing your story.

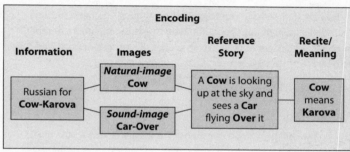

Figure 4.3 Encoding (2).

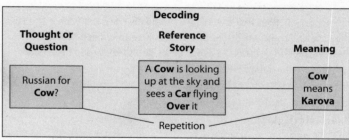

Figure 4.4 Decoding (2).

Selective memory and minimal images necessary (MIN)

In order for creative memorization to help us in our everyday life, progress our career or create expertise in a specific area, it is important to be selective about the information we encode by making sure that it is valuable to us in some way. There can be the temptation to create images for everything; however, this will most likely lead to a sense of frustration. It is therefore not only important but also advantageous to only encode the minimal number of images necessary to spark off the key information at a later date.

Key idea: MIN

In simple terms – if you already know it, then there's probably no need to encode. If one image can trigger off everything you need to know, then that's enough. Your goal should be to use the minimum number of images necessary in order to remember the key information and take some form of valuable action.

Remember this

One of the most common questions I have experienced across my career is, 'Isn't it easier just to remember the information rather than creating stories to represent them?' The answer to this will be different for every individual. If you find that you can remember text from books, facts, numbers, names, etc. without the need for any type of creative memorization, then that's what you should do. For most people this isn't the case and there will be specific areas where they need help or can improve. A good question to ask is 'What don't I know and how could creative memorization help?'

Dialling up

This is a simple technique you can use to dial up the intensity of your reference stories, making them bigger, brighter and more memorable. Initially, you can practise this with simple imagery and then move on to more complex reference stories.

Try it now: Dial up the apple

Time limit: 10 minutes

Imagine you have a dial with the numbers 1–10 either in front of you or on your wrist. Take a moment and imagine this dial in every detail:

* What is the shape of the face of the dial?
* What does the pointer of the dial look like?
* What is it made of?
* What colour is it?
* How does it feel?
* How big is it?
* Is it hot or cold?
* Does it get hotter the more you turn it up?
* Play with the dial, moving it up and down through the numbers 1–10.
* Do the numbers change colour as you do this?
* Do the numbers get bigger or smaller as you move up and down?
* Close your eyes and spend a few minutes seeing this dial in every detail, make it your dial, something you can use at any time to increase the intensity of the memories that you create.
* Now let us use the dial to intensify a simple image. Imagine that in front of you is an apple, just an ordinary apple. As you look at this apple you can see the dial moving on its own; if the image of the apple is not very clear, it will be drawn towards the 1, if it is bright and vibrant, if you can taste and feel it, if it is big and solid it will move towards the 10.
* As you look at the apple you watch where the dial rests, take control of the dial and very slowly move the dial all the way down. Notice what happens as you do this: does it become less clear? Do the colours drift away; perhaps it becomes black and white? Does it become more transparent or completely disappear? Take a moment and in your own time take control of the dial and move it slowly down to 1.
* Now in your own time, very slowly start to dial up the intensity of the apple, moving up through the numbers. Notice how the apple changes, notice how it grows bigger and brighter, more colourful and vibrant as you move up on your way to the higher numbers. Notice how real it becomes, until it's larger than life. Perhaps it actually comes to life? What happens as you move up to the number 10?

Spend a moment and enjoy the intensity of the memory you are creating.

✻ Finally, spend a few minutes moving the dial up and down. As you take complete control of your dial, notice how you can make the apple completely disappear or burst into life right in front of you.

Try using your dial with some of the reference stories you created for the countries and capitals. Run through the story in your mind and notice where the dial is. When you are ready, take control of the dial and move it up through the numbers – if it's on a 3, just move it to 5 initially and notice the difference in how clear the story seems. Then move it to 7, then 9, then 10. Run the story forwards and backwards a few times with the dial at a high number.

Remember this

Dialling up can be a very powerful tool. I tend to use it with information I wish to remember for long periods of time, or presentations which need to be locked in my mind and roll off the tongue. My suggestion would be to keep it simple in the beginning; when practising some of the sense memory exercises, see what happens when you dial them up.

Active daydreaming

Daydreaming can have a lot of negative associations: most people at some point in their lives have been told to 'stop daydreaming'. Perhaps people often referred to you as 'a daydreamer'. This usually implies that you have a lack of concentration and can't focus on what is 'really important'.

Daydreaming can be a very powerful skill. In essence, daydreaming is the ability to go into a trance state. You may have experienced this when driving your car and ending up at your destination not quite remembering the last five minutes, or sitting in a meeting room only to find that you've lost the thread of the conversation. More than likely it can happen when presentations are happening, and you find yourself doodling and going off on a journey in your mind.

Key idea: Active daydreaming

You can think of active daydreaming as the ability to lightly direct and guide your thoughts to produce positive results. It is the point where you become less aware of your conscious thoughts and have the ability to access your unconscious resources.

Remember this

As a hypnotherapist, I find it useful when guiding a person into trance to compare it to this daydreaming state as it is something that everyone has experienced and creates a clear point of reference as to what to expect when you are hypnotized. I personally find it useful to think of entering into this state when creating ideas, solving problems or creating reference stories.

Try it now: How many uses for a safety pin?

Time limit: 3 minutes

How many uses could there be for a safety pin? If there were no limits and the laws of physics didn't exist? Let yourself actively daydream on this thought after you've read through the process below.

* Ask yourself a question that guides you towards an outcome, i.e. What can I currently use a safety pin for? What can't I use a safety pin for? (If you can't use it to fly a plane, imagine how you might construct a network of safety pins that form the wheel and control panels.)
* 'Anything is possible', there is no 'cannot'.
* 'Expect' to get answers to your questions.
* Get yourself into a relaxed state of mind.
* Let your thoughts drift.
* As imagery and ideas pop into your mind, capture them in some way (mind maps and visual thinking are ideal for this – or just write the words, doodle and draw pictures).
* Continue to gently ask questions and let your mind drift. When your mind goes off at a tangent, enjoy the experience and know that your brain is searching for connections.

Case study: *Memory Masters* Countries and Capitals

Back in 1994 while preparing for one of the first meetings to pitch *Memory Masters* to the BBC, I came up with the idea of having the contestants memorize all of the world's countries and capitals. I had never attempted this before, so I had no idea whether it would be possible. A few of my friends volunteered to take part as the contestants for the pitch, and gave up a couple of days of their time to prepare. In advance of memorization I had created reference stories for all of the worlds countries and capitals as I believed this would speed up the process and really give the contestants a sense of what it felt like to memorize this much stuff. Over the course of those days I shared some of the core memory strategies and we spent about one of those days memorizing the countries and capitals. It seemed to go well, however I had no idea whether all of this would stick.

Come the day of the pitch it was time to see if this would work! The pair game was the second game in the format, it was a round on the buzzer and the contestants would put their knowledge into practice. The whole thing was pretty impressive, it almost seemed too easy for the contestants to remember the countries and capitals and it became a game of speed. It demonstrated to me the power of reference stories, even under pressure and hinted that there was much more scope to what a person could remember with these strategies.

In practice

Try it now: The capitals game
Time limit: 30 minutes

Use the time to create reference stories for the following 17 countries and capitals. This game pushes you to encode the information and produce reference stories as quickly as you can. You should aim to go faster than feels comfortable; if you get stuck, move on. There are examples you can use, although it will work better if you use your own.

* The first country is Burundi and its capital is Bujumbura. First create images to represent the information – these images do not have to be complex; they just have to be something that sparks off enough of the word to help you remember.

* Burundi sounds like Brandy (B ran dy): we will use this as our sound-image[s].

* Bujumbura sounds like BeeJambra (Bee Jam Bra): this is another sound-image[s].

* Now we create a reference story – imagine a large glass of Brandy is being drunk by a Bee covered in sticky Jam and wearing a pink Bra OR large glass of Brandy, Bee embedded on top, Jam in sides, Bra in middle.

* It is important to make this reference story feel real. Think of everything you have learned from creative memorization: engage all of your senses, exaggerate the size of the images, imagine this happening right in front of you, perhaps 'you' are the bee – play around and see what feels good. Abstract your own ideas, own the experience.

* As you imagine this reference story, actively test it – see the Brandy, then say the word Burundi, this will 'connect' the sound-image to the real word and will help consolidate the 'meaning'. Next see the Bee Jam bra and repeat the capital Bujumbura out loud. Make a physical action as you repeat the information and say the image.

* Repeat this process at least five times.

* Now see the reference story in reverse and say the capital first and which country it belongs to. By doing this you are creating more connections with the information.

* Finally, write down the country and its capital.

Sensory information Country – Capital	Integrate images [n]/[s]	Integrate reference story	Active testing
Burundi – Bujumbura	Brandy[s] – BeeJamBra[s]	a large glass of **Brandy** is being drunk by a **Bee** covered in sticky **Jam** and wearing a pink **Bra**	Burundi's capital is Bujumbura
Comoros – Moroni	Cameras[s] – Moron[s]	lots of **Cameras** being used by a **Moron**	Comoros's capital is Moroni
Djibouti – Djibouti	JBoot[s]	2 **Boots** that are in the shape of a **J**	Djibouti's capital is Djibouti
Eritrea – Asmara	AirTree[s] – Asthma[s]	a tree is trying to get some air **AirTree** as it is suffering from **Asthma**	Eritrea's capital is Asmara
Ethiopia – Addis Ababa	Ethiopia[n] – AdidasBaby[n]	an Adidas Baby in Ethiopia	Ethiopia's capital is Addis Ababa
Kenya – Nairobi	Can[s] – NoRobe[s]	a **Can** covering up someone you know with **No Robes**	Kenya's capital is Nairobi
Madagascar – Antananarivo	Lion (Alex)[n] – Antenna[s]	**Alex the Lion** from Madagascar is wearing an **Antenna** on his head	Madagascar's capital is Antananarivo
Malawi – Lilongwe	MaleLawWee[s] – LongWee[s]	a **Male** who is involved in **Law** having a **Long Wee**	Malawi's capital is Lilongwe
Mauritania – Nouakchott	MoriartyTan[s] – KnockShot[s]	Moriarty has a Tan and Knocks before taking a Shot at Holmes	Mauritania's capital is Nouakchott
Mozambique – Maputo	MossBeak[s] – MyPutter[s]	a bird with a **MossBeak** is eating **MyPutter**	Mozambique's capital is Maputo
Rwanda – Kigali	Rwand[s] – Giggly[s]	a wizard is holding an **R wand** and is very **Giggly**	Rwanda's capital is Kigali
Seychelles – Victoria	SeaShells[s] – Victoria[n]	**SeaShells** are being made into a statue of **Queen Victoria**	Seychelles's capital is Victoria
Somalia – Mogadishu	Semolina[s] – MuckyDish[s]	left over **Semolina** has made a **MuckyDish**	Somalia's capital is Mogadishu
Tanzania – Dar-es-Salaam	Tasmanian devil[n] – DoorsSlam[s]	**Tasmanian devil** in a hall full of **Doors Slamming** them	Tanzania's capital is Dar-es-Salaam

Uganda – Kampala	UGun[s] – CampPole[s]	a **UGun** (gun in the shape of a U) blasts a **CampPole**	Uganda's capital is Kampala
Zambia – Lusaka	ZoomBeer[s] – LooSack[s]	a **Zoom**ing **Beer** falls into a **LooSack**	Zambia's capital is Lusaka
Zimbabwe – Harare	ZoomBaby[s] – Hairy[s]	a **Zoom**ing **Baby** is very **Hairy**	Zimbabwe's capital is Harare

Remember this

It has been my experience that when a person starts using creative memorization and creating reference stories, at first it can feel like a real challenge. This is why I have found it extremely beneficial with the people I have worked with to give them lots of examples to get them started. In the beginning, it is more important to create speed and see the results to keep motivation up than being able to encode your own images and reference stories, although ultimately this is the goal.

Focus points

✳ Encoding is used to convert information into memorable images that reference real information.

✳ Decoding is used to understand the meaning of images in a reference story (this is usually instant).

✳ Visual embedding is a process where you use the same sequence and pattern to encode a set of images, left to right or top to bottom.

✳ Narratives are a process of making information memorable by creating micro-stories, sometimes using something previously related to the word and changing the context.

✳ Aim to look for the value in what you are memorizing and use the Minimal Images Necessary (MIN) strategy to remember the information.

✳ Practise the dialling up technique to increase the intensity and memorability of your reference stories.

✳ Play with active daydreaming when you are looking for ways to create reference stories and tap into your creative unconscious resources.

Next steps

By increasing your expertise at bringing anything you want to remember to life with all of your senses, you will naturally create memorable experiences. Look for opportunities to generate small reference stories for things that you would find valuable to remember. Start small, something someone mentioned in a conversation, the name of a person in an article or a task you need to do later that day.

5

The chain method: Build your capacity to remember

In this chapter you will learn:

▶ *benefits of using the chain method*
▶ *guiding principles to make information stick*
▶ *real-world examples of the chain method.*

The chain method is a core memory technique. It is quite probable that you have experienced it in one form or another or heard its name. If so, you may have already built up some associations and thoughts about its use, the challenges and practical applications.

In this chapter we will focus on the chain method's guiding principles and practical use and challenge you to 'search for where it can add value' within your own world.

Case study: 60 items in 60 minutes

Back in the early 90s when I first started running training on memory techniques, I would start the morning by having everyone in the session just focus on the Chain Method. There is a temptation with memory strategies to try and cram in everything too quickly before really getting a grasp of the basics AND becoming good at them.

In those morning sessions I would break down in some detail how to use the chain method and have everyone try to put it into practice. By the end of the morning 'every single person in the room' usually around 50 people would be able to recite each of the items forwards and backwards in sequence. I would also call out an item and have them tell me which items were before and after. Before being exposed to training in memory techniques, for most people this would seem an impossible task.

The outcome is that every single person was able to experience what it felt like to remember this much information in such a short time scale. The thing to note is that the information itself was fairly irrelevant (random words), however the framework for remembering this much information was, for many, transformational.

Take the 60 items in 60 minutes memory challenge now: http://improve-your-memory-memoryschool.com

Link by link

A major benefit of the chain method (sometimes referred to as the link system or link method) is that it allows you to take small chunks of related or non-related information and sequentially link them together for storage in mid- to long-term memory. This core technique extends the principle of reference stories. You might think of a chain method story as large reference stories with anything between 10 and 20 images.

Remember this

Essentially reference stories, link systems and chain methods are the same thing. I have referred to them by these names to help identify their purpose. I personally use the term 'reference story' for small chunks of information that are self-contained – a country and capital, English word and foreign equivalent, or a historic fact and date are examples of these. My preference for chain method stories is to remember lists of sequential items that won't change – chapters in a book or directions along a route, etc.

Try it now: Fact or fiction?

Time limit: 10 minutes

* Think about the natural process that happens when you read an engaging fictional book: how much do you remember? Do you recall the sequence of events? Details of the characters?
* Choose a fictional book that comes to mind and take three minutes to write down either in note form, pictures, story boards or on a mind map how much detail you can remember of it. Who were the characters? What was the plot? And so on...
* Now think back to the last factual book you read and write down as many details as you can.
* How were the experiences different? Did you find you remembered more of the fictional book in sequence or more details? In the factual book, if a key fact stood out, what was it about it that made it memorable?
* Capture your results and identify how you could make the factual book more memorable.

When you read the fictional book, chances are you were not making a conscious effort to remember. However, if the plot is vivid enough, it becomes instinctively more memorable, to the point where you can remember sequences of events in great detail. You are able to recall the experiences as if they were real and extract semantic information such as places, characters, dates and specific factual dialogue.

This is not always the way with a factual book: even if there is comprehension of semantic information, these facts can seem to fade from our memory. It is not linked to an experience, is probably difficult to remember in sequence or even at all until questioned later, at which time it may pop back into your mind if there was a strong enough meaning and association. One benefit of the chain method is the ability to create memorable experiences with semantic information.

The principles

There are some useful principles to abide by when using the chain method. These principles are within the context of the four core skills of creative memorization – flow, imagination, association and meaning.

SET THE BACKDROP

When you first start using the chain method, your chains can feel like they are floating in the ether of your mind, set against a backdrop of white or black, not connected to any specific location. Sometimes this can work, other times this can lead to similar images in different chains becoming confused, or just a general lack of clarity.

Just as you would set the backdrop within a book, a play or a movie, it helps to set the backdrop for the stories that you create in your mind. This backdrop can act as an anchor for the chains you create and a 'way in' to the story.

If I were to memorize the main topics in a book about programming, my backdrop may be the PHP conference I attended in California a few years back (note: although the backdrop is a point of reference, this is not the same as filing systems which we will discuss in the next chapter). I would perhaps imagine the story happening inside the hotel lobby or within a conference room or I may use the office I remember from the film *The Social Network*. I could even construct an imaginary stage (literally) within a theatre and on the stage are desks in a circle with laptops being powered by robots; this is where my story will take place.

Once my backdrop is set, I prime myself to think about the backdrop whenever I think about the book. I do this with some simple visualization and repetition – see the book, think about the backdrop, see the book, think about the backdrop, repeat this for about 60 seconds and the two are interlinked. Once the backdrop is primed, I am ready to create my chain of links.

HOW BIG SHOULD THE CHAIN BE?
The length of the chain depends on the type of information, your proficiency and how memorable you make it. Short chains – five links work well, however, you can just as easily use 10 or 20 if the information is contained and doesn't change. You should experiment and find out what works well for you.

Once you start – don't stop! Drive forward…

When you begin creating your links, focus on speed initially, build up a sense of rhythm and do not over-analyse. If you try to perfect each image before moving on, or have everything make sense, you are likely to get tired or lose motivation. When the information is more complex, this can lead to reverting back to simple rote memorization.

Remember this

Most people will have experienced this state at some point in their lives, when a person is in the 'state of flow', perhaps playing a sport, giving a presentation, playing a blinding shot on a pool table or on the tennis court or coming up with a new idea in a meeting that everyone starts going along with. If you have experienced this in the past, you will remember that you have a feeling of just going with it, of momentum – this is the feeling that you want to let happen when using creative memorization and in this context the chain method.

DIALLING UP THE INTENSITY
This is the same technique used in the previous chapter: use your dial to intensify the experience and create vibrant, alive images and experiences.

REMOTE CONTROL

Once you have completed all the links in your chain and you have a story built up in your mind, run it through as if you were fast forwarding a movie using a remote control. Play it forward about 5–10 times, building up a sense of rhythm, intensifying the experience and involving all of your senses. Once you are confident with the sequence, press rewind and run the movie backwards, experiencing everything in reverse.

FAST FORWARD AND REWIND

When you are happy that you can play the story in both directions, take it to the next level and hit fast forward and fast rewind. Run it forwards and backwards on high speed for 1–2 minutes. By running these patterns in this way, you will help strengthen the synaptic connections and create a solid chain.

ACT OUT!

This is where you get to actively test the information you have memorized. It is an essential step, especially when remembering speeches or presentations. As you watch the movie, narrate the real information, feel free to dramatize this – use physical gestures as if you were giving a speech to an audience or telling the story to a group of children. Recite the information in different genres – as if you were telling a horror, a drama, a comedy, a melodrama. Play with it and make it your own.

REVISION

Revision is important to condition the connections you have made, as mentioned in the first chapter. The suggested pattern for this is one hour after initial memorization, then one day, one week, one month, three months, six months, then as needed. In real terms the amount of revision will depend on the importance of the material and how you use it, along with how strong your initial connections are.

Remember this

In the beginning make a conscious effort to apply all the guiding principles. If you do this, in time it will start to happen naturally. By working in this way, you will build up good habits and a solid foundation, allowing you to use your skills for more complex information.

Building the chain

If chain methods and reference stories are going to be useful to you in your life, your brain and, more specifically, your neurons need to get used to creating these types of pattern, so you no longer have to consciously think about 'how' you might create a connection and your unconscious can just throw out ideas and do the hard work for you.

On starting the journey to building up these patterns of a new way of thinking, work through these 'actions', creating your own links wherever possible.

Try it now: Ten elements
Time limit: 5 minutes

Follow the guiding principles to remember the first ten elements of the periodic table:

* Set the backdrop – perhaps you see a laboratory; the story below will happen with this backdrop. Throughout the story the backdrop may change to reflect the action.

* Create an image for each word in your mind (natural-image [n] and sound-image [s]):

    1 Hydrogen – Bomb [n]
    2 Helium – Balloon [n]
    3 Lithium – Leaves [s]
    4 Beryllium – Bee [s]
    5 Boron – Boar [s]
    6 Carbon – Car [s]
    7 Nitrogen – Nitro [s]
    8 Oxygen – Oxygen mask [n]
    9 Fluorine – Toothpaste [n]

* Neon – Neon strip [n] Make the images come alive; use your sense memory.

* Create your links to form a story using your imagination and association.

Example

You walk into the laboratory holding a Bomb and throw it into a hot air Balloon. As it rises and explodes, thousands of green Leaves fall to the ground covering a Bee (the size of a person), which stings a Boar. The boar runs at you and you manage to get into a Car before it smashes the door. You press the big button that says Nitro, you are going so fast around the laboratory an Oxygen mask drops down. When you stop, you take the huge tube of Toothpaste from the dashboard, step outside and squirt it onto a Neon strip.

* Dial up the intensity.
* Use the movie method.
* Act out! – The first few times you can recite the story you created. After that just recite the 'real' information – Hydrogen, Helium, Lithium, etc. while seeing the story in your mind.

Try it now: Book challenge
Time limit: 5 minutes

Here is an example of how you might use the chain method to quickly memorize the table of contents of a book. The book in this example is *Getting To Yes – Negotiating an agreement without giving in* by Roger Fisher and William Ury.

Here are the eight main content areas of the book, with examples of some images:
* Don't bargain over positions – lotus position
* Separate the people from the problem – people, problem blob
* Focus on interests, not positions – interesting sweets
* Invent options for mutual gain – invent options under three cups
* Insist on objective criteria – little critter
* Develop your BATNA (best alternative to negotiated agreement) – a BAT
* Negotiation Jujitsu – jujitsu
* Taming the hard bargainer – Taming

Remember to go through each stage of the guiding principles.

Try to have just one image representing each of the phrases. Before going on to create the chain method story, make sure you encode each of the sentences. When you see that Lotus position in your mind, you have to know that it means 'Don't bargain over positions'. This will make it a lot easier to recite the real information after you have linked together the whole chain.

Example

Reagan and Gorbachev are standing across from each other in the White House (my backdrop). I am sitting in a lotus position, they start fighting so I fly through the air and try to separate these people from a problem blob covering them. My focus is drawn to some interesting sweets stuck to the middle of Gorbachev's head. I grab the sweet and invent a game where I put the sweet under one of three cups, giving them options to choose from. An objective little critter jumps on top of cups and is holding a large metal bat, and starts hitting Reagan and Gorbachev, who join forces and do some jujitsu moves on the little critter, taming it and putting it back into its cage before shaking hands.

Although there is not a lot of detail here, this chain method story acts as a reference that lets me understand the essence of what the book is about. My brain will naturally reflect on information I already know about this subject and is primed for new input. Even without reading any more I, could have a conversation with someone about it and explore what I think each section means from my own experience. It will also clarify my purpose, i.e. What level of detail do I now want from this book? What are the key areas of interest for me? What will I do with this information?

Try it now: *Improve Your Memory* chain method story
Time limit: 10 minutes

Preview the index of this book and extract a main key word for each chapter title and use the link system to form a chain that will act as your reference story for this book.

Remember to use the core principles of creative memorization and go through each of the guiding principles of the chain method.

Focus points

* The chain method allows you to store potentially unrelated information in long-term memory.
* The chain method is like a long reference story.
* When using the chain method, put the information you are memorizing in context by giving it a backdrop.
* Aim to keep the size of your chain between 5 and 20 links.
* Create your links quickly and don't over-think; drive forward the momentum to keep your motivation levels high.
* Use the dialling up technique to intensify the memory of your chain.
* Practise using the 'remote control' – run your chain forwards and backwards in your mind to consolidate it to long-term memory.
* Act out! Test that you remember all the information in your chain.
* Review your chains from time to time, one hour after memorization, then one day, one week, one month, as and when.

Next steps

Think about this, if you could make it a habit to implement the chain method in social conversations, key points from meetings or rapidly capture the main themes of presentations and books, what impact would that have for you in your life?

The chain method is about much more than just remembering shopping lists, it's a core ability that can transform how you learn.

6

Memory networks: Your limitless mental storage systems

In this chapter you will learn:

► *how to organize your information through classification*

► *making information easier to remember by chunking*

► *how to store information in a structured manner*

► *techniques for creating limitless mental filing systems*

► *get into the moment with your iMind*

► *how to use mental filing systems in the real world.*

In this chapter you will discover how to use your skills to construct memory networks to store and retrieve an almost unlimited amount of information.

Case study: The World Memory Championships

One of the toughest mental challenges was competing in the 1995 World Memory Championships. While I had been using these memory strategies for a few years, I had never competed, however during a conversation with Tony Buzan he convinced me I should come along and give it a go! Not one to say no I thought I'd give it a shot. The next three months were pretty full on and I did about four hours training a day. One of the key skills was building up memory networks or memory palaces in my mind to store the huge amount of information I was going to attempt to remember in those two days of competition.

The results changed my beliefs about what I and others are actually capable of after memorizing 732 digits in one hour, 312 cards in one hour and 905 binary digits in 30 minutes as well as many other memory feats. The outcome was that I was one of the first Grand Masters of Memory in the world. The strategy you are about to learn will give you the ability to do all of this and so much more.

Classification

Key idea: Classification

'The action or process of classifying something according to similar qualities or characteristics.'

Before digging into the workings of memory networks, it is beneficial to spend some time thinking about the classification and chunking of information.

One of the most challenging areas when starting a new job, learning a new subject or developing a new skill is knowing how to classify your information. Where do you start? What do you read? What do you need to learn and remember first? What is the best way to group the information? The answers to these questions will have an impact on 'what' you memorize, 'when' you memorize and 'how' you memorize. Your approach should involve classifying your information in line with your outcomes.

RECOGNIZING PATTERNS

For our purposes classification involves recognizing patterns that allow you to group similar information so it is easier to remember.

Think of the last time you walked into a bookshop. You immediately notice that the books have been classified into genres – fiction, science, children's, etc. Within those sections they are further classified alphabetically. This means that your brain can quickly identify those patterns within the shop; each genre has a specific location, making it easy to remember. If your outcome was to develop your management skills for the purpose of building a high-performing team, you may head to the business and self-development sections – there could be useful information in both these places.

▶ Slicing

To help with recognizing patterns, a simple technique is to think of vertical and horizontal slices.

You might imagine a vertical slice being the table of contents within a book. If you were to memorize this, you would build up a big picture view of knowledge across the whole subject of the book.

You could imagine a horizontal slice consisting of one specific topic either within one book or across several books. To memorize this will increase the detail of knowledge on that one topic.

Let us visualize this in the context of a set of four books on memory improvement:

▶ *Improve Your Memory* (Mark Channon)

▶ *How to Pass Exams* (Dominic O'Brien)

▶ *Develop a Perfect Memory* (Tony Buzan)

▶ *Moonwalking with Einstein* (Joshua Foer)

Your purpose is to know as much about 'improving your memory' as possible, so you decide that you will take both vertical and horizontal slices from each book. The vertical slices will give you the big picture and the horizontal slices will give you the detail.

For each book the category for the vertical slice could be classified as the author. When you think of an author, you get back the name of the book along with the table of contents, topics and some main facts.

For each book you will have horizontal slices that could be classified by topics of interest. Let us say 'remembering names' was a topic you wanted to become an expert on. You extract details from each of the relevant chapters within the book and across all of the books; perhaps you also research what is on the internet and buy some more books giving more insights. This will build up a detailed view of that horizontal slice.

Both vertical and horizontal slices are done in the context of the learning cycle – you consume sensory information, reflect on what you know (which is increasing with each vertical or horizontal slice), abstract your own ideas and take action. You become excellent at remembering names and have a solid knowledge about improving your memory in general that you can use in your everyday life.

Of course you could just as easily choose to take a horizontal slice on its own. You want to remember names, so you consume a chapter from one book, reflect, abstract and put it into practice; this is a small horizontal slice. If you consume the chapters on names from four books, you have a bigger horizontal slice and potentially a more detailed view on that topic.

Thinking back to the bookshop analogy, your purpose was to learn about building a 'high performing team'. In this scenario you may take a horizontal slice from books across the two genres – business and self-development – extracting key information and creating your own classification called 'high-performing teams'.

As you will find out, we can create memory networks in our mind that mirror these classifications, building up storage structures for easy retrieval of information.

Remember this

There can be a temptation with memory techniques to try to 'remember everything'. I've experienced this myself and your productivity can suffer. You don't have to remember 'everything'; however, you do want to remember 'anything' that will add value to your outcomes. If you already know something, don't waste time on rebuilding the memory with a memory technique. In this fast-paced world make the most of your time by classifying and remembering the things that allow you to be most effective.

Try it now: Classify me!

Time limit: 5 minutes
* Think about an area in which you wish to learn to develop your skills.
* What is most important for you to learn? What are you going to want to put into practice first? What is most important to you, and why?
* Reflect and abstract how you might slice up and classify this information.
* Write down or visually represent your findings.

Chunking

Once you have classified your information and are at a more granular level, you can start to look at the best way of organizing the information into bite-size chunks that are easier to remember and you can use for reference stories.

Key idea: Chunking

Chunking is a fairly simple concept and a way of taking a collection of data and breaking it down so it can be more manageable for our working memory.

The classic example of this is a number: 241849382. On its own it seems pretty unwieldy to process; however, chunk it up and it is easier for your working memory to manage, i.e. 241, 849, 382 – you can hold these numbers in your mind long enough to work with them, think what they mean, how you might use them, etc.

Continuing with the bookshop analogy, if you extracted information from a chapter in, let's say, Ken Blanchard's *The One Minute Manager Builds High Performing Teams*, you might take the chunk of information that represents what a high performing team looks like at a high level by memorizing the mnemonic PERFORM:

▶ Purpose

▶ Empowerment

▶ Relationships

▶ Flexibility

▶ Optimal performance

▶ Recognition

▶ Morale

You could also have a reference story (chain) to give a clearer picture of what the word PERFORM represents if it helps:

Imagine a PERFORMER with a real PURPOSE and super POWERS, in an intimate RELATIONSHIP with the OPTIMAL product (iPad), that has facial RECOGNITION and makes her feel GREAT.

Networks

Memory networks are a way of thinking about a group of systems that grew from the art of memory, allowing a structured approach to storing and retrieving the information you have classified.

Key idea: Memory networks

A memory network is built up of unique nodes that follow a sequence and potentially point to other memory networks. The way you slice, classify and chunk your information will have an impact on how you construct your memory networks. As you continue to read, think about how you might construct your own.

There are a variety of memory networks. Here is a list of the most well-known:

▶ Peg lists – the body system, the rhyme system, the number shape system

▶ Method of loci – the journey method, the Roman room method (item system) or memory palace

▶ The major or phonetic system (also used for numbers).

They all follow the same process for storing information:

1 Identify a network of images (these are your nodes) that follow a sequence (parts of your body, pictures that rhyme with numbers, items in your home, locations along a route, etc.).

2 Memorize the sequence of your nodes.

3 Connect the information you want to remember to your nodes.

Remember this

The term 'memory network' is not a 'new system'; it is merely a way of referring to any memory technique that allows you to mentally store information. My purpose here is to create a common language for us to share the various applications of memory networks throughout the book. In the same way a 'node' can represent a location on a journey, an item in your home or a picture in a number shape system. Memory networks also conjure up imagery of neuronal networks in your mind with the idea that a memory network can mirror those internal synaptic connections.

THE PEG LIST

One of the simplest examples of a memory network is the peg list, the idea that you can 'hang' items off a virtual peg. In real terms you are simply creating an association between the peg (node) and the item you wish to remember.

The body system is a straightforward example of a peg list:

- ▶ Feet
- ▶ Knees
- ▶ Thighs
- ▶ Behind
- ▶ Waist
- ▶ Chest
- ▶ Neck
- ▶ Face
- ▶ Hair
- ▶ Ceiling

As you can see, it uses different parts of the body for visual pegs; associating information you wish to remember with each one of these images allows you to memorize rapidly and recall in or out of sequence.

 Try it now: How to memorize a memory network
Time limit: 5 minutes

Memorization of a memory network is a simple process. The following steps you go through relate to all types of memory network:
1 Get yourself into a relaxed and focused state.
2 Imagine your first image vividly and say the name of the node aloud.
3 Repeat this process for each node of the memory network.
4 Now do this process in reverse.
5 Repeat steps 2–4 three times.
6 Chunk the files into smaller groups (1–5, for example).
7 Use the movie method – run through each group forwards and backwards in your mind as quickly as you can.
8 Use the movie method – run through the whole network forwards and backwards as quickly as you can until you are sure of the sequence in your memory network.

CLEANING A MEMORY NETWORK

You may have memory networks that you use repeatedly for simple tasks. You could think of these as temporary memory networks, i.e. they have not been designed with a specific purpose of storing key information you wish to transfer to your long-term memory. With such a memory network you do not want to store the information any longer than is needed to complete your task.

If we use the simple example of storing a list of 'things to do', once you have completed the list you have no more use for this information. By simply leaving the memory networks for a few days, you will find that the images fade considerably; this is mainly due to the fact that when you memorized them, your intention was only to keep them for a short period of time, therefore your connections were less intense and therefore less memorable. After a few days you can go ahead and use the same system to store similar types of information.

There are times when images get 'stuck' or maybe you want to use the same memory network before the images have had time to fade. In this scenario there is a way of dulling down and erasing the information you associate with your files.

To clean a memory network, create an eraser image; this could be cellophane, for example, it is clear and has a feeling of nothingness, and gives the effect of erasing. Wrap the cellophane around each one of your files and say the word 'erase'.

▶ Rhyme list and number shape system

Other peg lists include the rhyme list and number shape system; these also have some simple applications when it comes to remembering numbers, which we will look at in a later section.

Steps in creating a rhyme list and number shape system

Simply create an image that rhymes with each number from 0 to 10:

0 Hero

1 Bun

2 Shoe

3 Tree

4 Door

5 Hive

6 Sticks

7 Heaven

8 Plate

9 Wine

10 Hen

For the number shape system create an image that looks like the number:

0 Polo

1 Pencil

2 Swan

3 Bum

4 Sail

5 Hook

6 Bag

7 Nose

8 Track

9 Balloon

10 Laurel & Hardy

Try it now: Your daily meetings
Time limit: 5 minutes

An application of these systems is in helping to remember the order of your daily meetings. The value of this will of course depend on how busy you are.

Although this information can be stored on your phone, tablet or laptop, having this knowledge at your fingertips can create a sense of certainty and control in knowing what is coming up next, especially if you are working back to back.

Ideally you would take five minutes at the beginning of each day to memorize the sequence of meetings.

Memorize the following fictitious meetings:
✳ Catch up with one of your team members
✳ A project review with your manager
✳ Phone call with a potential client
✳ Meeting with a designer over new designs of your website
✳ Lunch with a colleague
✳ Your monthly stakeholder meeting
✳ Offsite meeting in Starbucks
✳ Email catch-up
✳ Work on an idea for a new project
✳ Business dinner at local restaurant (or pub)
Daily meetings example

Imagine the scenario in the location that it is happening and associate the rhyme list images or number shape images – take no more than two minutes. This technique can be done at high speed as the associations are fairly simple.
✳ *Your team member is eating a massive **bun**.*
✳ *Your manager is in the room where you are meeting him wearing massive clown **shoes** (this may also change your perception and your state).*
✳ *Your potential client is on the phone up a **tree**.*
✳ *Your designer is painting the **door** of the location where you are meeting him.*
✳ *You are having lunch with your colleague surrounded by **bees**.*
✳ *In your stakeholder meeting they are all holding big **sticks**!*
✳ *Imagine an **angel** in Starbucks.*
✳ *You are catching emails on your **plate** at your desk.*
✳ *Pouring **wine** over your new project.*
✳ *At dinner with lots of **hens**.*

By taking a few minutes each day to create some simple associations, you can remain focused and make sure you are prepared for the next meeting. The value of this technique will vary, depending on your career.

Remember this

You will notice that I haven't added any times to these meetings. Since meetings are generally either 30 minutes or one hour, sometimes this is not needed. If you want to add in times, the upcoming number systems are ideal for this type of scenario. If using the above method, I would recommend alternating between the rhyme list and number shape system daily. This will allow the images to fade.

THE METHOD OF LOCI

The method of loci follows the simple principle of associating information you wish to remember with well-known 'locations' throughout some kind of journey; the locations are your 'nodes'.

The nodes may be simple items in your home, as with the Roman room method and memory palace, or points of focus on a journey from your home to work, sometimes referred to as the journey system. It may also be a combination of both.

In the following sections you will create three different memory networks using the method of loci. The first will use the Roman room method or memory palace, the second will use the journey method and the third will be one of your choice.

You will put these memory networks into practice at the end of this chapter by memorizing 60 key management models.

Try it now: Creating your memory palace
Time limit: 5 minutes

Create 20 locations using a memory palace (also known as Roman room method).

* To create a memory palace, you first need to choose a place that is your palace. For this action I would suggest you choose your home.
* Imagine you enter through the front door of your home (your memory palace). As you walk through your palace, 'note' the first four rooms you come to and their sequence.
* From each room within your palace you are going to choose just five items. Imagine picking the first item on your left and looking around

the room in a 'clockwise' direction, choose the next four items that follow in sequence – these items are your visual 'nodes' – you may have something like: chair, curtains, table, TV and bookcase.

✵ Choose five items from each room.

✵ Write the rooms and items in the table below.

Room 1	Room 2
1	6
2	7
3	8
4	9
5	10

Room 3	Room 4
11	16
12	17
13	18
14	19
15	20

Use the steps in *How to Memorize a Memory Network* in the 'Try it now' box from earlier in this chapter.

A memory palace doesn't have to be in your home; you could use your office, a bar or restaurant – as long as you have a room, all you have to do is select items from that room in a clockwise order as your visual nodes. Don't worry about knowing what the numbers are; the important thing is to remember their sequence.

THE JOURNEY METHOD

The journey method is another name for a memory network that utilizes the method of loci. Its advantage over some other memory networks is that you can generally construct very large networks and therefore hold a lot of information while still memorizing at a high speed.

It is based on the principle of selecting different locations as your visual nodes along a particular journey. You pick a starting location and a finishing location, and then choose as many locations in between as you can think of. The locations themselves can be anything – a room, a hallway, a garden, the corner of a street, a bus stop, a bus or a tree in a park; basically your location is any area of space that you can instantly recognize. It is important that you focus on a particular point at each location.

An example of a 'journey' might be a journey from your home to your work. You do not need to remember the numbers of your nodes, just the order in which they appear. Let's take a look at a hypothetical illustration:

▶ Home

▶ Garden

▶ Car

▶ Corner with a lamp

▶ Fence

▶ Chemist

▶ Roundabout

▶ Tesco

▶ Train entrance

▶ Inside station

▶ Tube stairs...

You will continue creating locations until you get to your office.

Remember this

I find that the best way to create a new journey is to choose the start and end points; you can then take your journey and fill in the gaps. If you need a total of 50 locations and you end up with only 30, you can go back through the journey looking for locations you might have missed out. For example, there may have been a newsagent in between 'inside station' and the 'tube stairs', so you could add this in. If needed, you can extend the journey – office to coffee shop, etc.

Try it now: Building a journey
Time limit: 5 minutes

Create 30 locations using the journey method. You may find that you end up with many more locations than that. It is all right if you do; for the 'Try it now' towards the end of this chapter we shall just use the first 30.

* Name your journey – if it is a journey from home to work, call it home–work.
* Choose your start and end locations.
* Take no more than 10 minutes to brainstorm all of the locations in between. Make your locations as close together as possible as this will make for easier memorization.
* Use the steps in *How to Memorize a Memory Network* from earlier in this chapter.

You can create as many journeys as your imagination and memory will allow; you may want to think of journeys you have taken throughout your life – to your school or college, to old places of work, airports, restaurants, places on holidays or trips to beaches. There are literally thousands of locations you could create.

Remember this

Over the years I have noticed that creating memory networks has become a blocker for many people. They feel challenged thinking about new journeys, or simply feel they don't have the time. Using Google Maps streetview is a great way to rapidly create almost limitless memory networks.

THE iMIND

While working with clients I will often ask the question, "where do you see experiences in your mind? Inside your head? Out in front of you? Far away in a different location?"

As you might expect, it seems that many people do all of these. What's interesting is that 'where' people see these experiences seems to have an impact on the task they are performing. For example while working with clients on presentations or talks who are using a chain method, if those experiences are somewhere at the back of their mind they seem more likely to 'lose' their place as they are temporarily taken 'out of the moment' and 'remember' the next image in the chain'.

In contrast those who learn to project those experiences out in front of them (imagining a scene in *The Avengers* where Tony Stark works with Holographic displays) are much more 'in the moment' and less likely to lose where they are, since they can immediately see and touch the next image in the sequence.

This mode of being 'in the moment' and not 'remembering' is a useful one to consider when putting the chain method (or any other memory strategy) into practice. I call this the iMind strategy, as you are interacting with the projections in your mind.

▶ **iMind strategy**

There are five steps to using the iMind strategy

1 Project any images you have created out into the space in front of you

2 Make them as visual and physical as possible

3 Dial them up, bigger, brighter and tactile

4 Choose between the chain method or memory network. If you are in a room you can create a memory network on the fly, otherwise chain the key images together. Throw your images onto your files after you create them or throw them out there as you chain them together (think about those scenes in *The Avengers* ☺)

5 Practise playing back out loud what they mean and being completely in the moment

Try it now: using your iMind

The best way to start using your iMind is with simple items, so you really get a feeling for how it works. Put it into practice with these simple items:

✱ Mouse, Easel, Typewriter, Trampoline, Washing basket
✱ Go through each of the five steps

Remember this

From here on in, think about whether the thing you want to remember would benefit from using the iMind strategy, there are no right or wrong rules here, experiment and see what works best for you. You may find that when you are constructing reference stories it helps to use your iMind and then mentally transfer them to a memory network somewhere in your mind.

In practice

THE KEY MANAGEMENT MODELS

The application of memory networks is invaluable: they allow you to memorize high volumes of information and at high speed. The speed at which you can memorize information makes them an essential and practical tool when it comes to helping you to progress your career through education or in business.

In order to understand how to put your memory networks into use and to demonstrate the value of working with them, try spending some time using the three filing systems you have created to remember the 60 key management models from Assen, Berg and Pietersma's *Key Management Models*. We will classify the management models into strategic, tactical and operational; we will need the following number of nodes (files):

▶ 18 files to remember the strategic models in the first system

▶ 30 files to remember the tactical models in the second system

▶ 12 files to remember the operational models in the third system.

Taking a vertical slice from the book, you will memorize the names of each of these models.

In order to comprehend how these models work, you have to experience them and put them into practice. By remembering the names of each of the management models you are effectively creating points of reference within your mind for each of the models.

Remember this

When I first memorized these models, it took only 60 minutes to commit the names of the models to memory — it took a further two weeks playing with each model to understand it. This is a relatively short space of time and for me has value. I noticed from a leadership point of view to have Covey's seven habits as a reference was invaluable when working with my team. It may be that you choose the models that are most relevant to you. What is your top ten that you can use to help make an impact in your career?

▶ Strategic models

Memory network node (location)	Sensory information management model	Integrate reference story (examples)
	Ansoff's product / market grid	Ants on a market
	The BCG matrix	Boston red soxs Consulting
	Blue ocean strategy	Blue Ocean
	Competitive analysis: Porter's five forces	A hand with five fingers being competitive
	Core competencies	Apple core
	Greiner's growth model	Grinding a model
	Kay's distinctive capabilities	Kay is very distinctive
	Market-driven organization	A market driving
	Off-shoring / outsourcing	Off-shore shipping truck
	Road-mapping	A road map
	Scenario planning	A crazy scenario
	Strategic dialogue	Two very strategic people having dialogue
	Strategic HRM model	Human Resources making models
	Strategic human capital planning	Humans on the capital planning
	SWOT analysis	A SWATter
	The value chain	Expensive valuable chain
	Value-based management	Valuable basin with management inside
	The value disciplines of Treacy and Wiersema	Dick Tracy Fears Semolina

▶ Tactical models

Memory network node (location)	Sensory information management model	Integrate reference story (your stories)
	The 7-S framework	
	Activity-based costing	
	Beer and Nohria – E and O theories	
	Benchmarking	
	Business process redesign	
	Competing values of organizational effectiveness	
	Core quadrants	
	Covey's seven habits of highly effective people	
	Curry's pyramid: customer marketing and relationship management	
	The DuPont analysis	
	Factory gate pricing	
	Henderson and Venkatraman's strategic alignment model	
	Hofstede's cultural dimensions	
	House of purchasing and supply	
	The innovation circle	
	Kotler's 4Ps of marketing	
	Kotler's eight phases of change	
	Kraljic's purchasing model	
	Lean thinking / just-in-time	
	MABA analysis	
	Milkovich's compensation model	
	Mintzberg's configurations	
	Monczka's purchasing model	
	Overhead value analysis	
	Quick response manufacturing	
	Senge – the fifth discipline	
	Six Sigma	
	The EFQM excellence model	
	The theory of constraints	
	Vendor managed inventory	

► Operational models

Memory network node (location)	Sensory information management model	Integrate reference story (your stories)
	The balanced scorecard (BSC)	
	Belbin's team roles	
	The branding pentagram	
	Change quadrants	
	Discounted cashflow	
	Kaizen / Gemba	
	Mintzberg's management roles	
	Risk reward analysis	
	Root cause analysis / Pareto analysis	
	The six thinking hats of de Bono	
	The Deming cycle: plan-do-check-act	
	Value stream mapping	

Remember this

The method of loci memory networks are extremely effective once you have had time to practise with them. They can be used in isolation or combined together to create more complex networks. The inside of shops along a street could be used to hold main chapters of a book and items within those shops could be used for details of that chapter. You can use it to remember an almost limitless variety of things – dance steps, speeches, books and as mentioned even games for the World Memory Championships; with it the current record holder Simon Reinhard can do the same thing in 20.44 seconds (2015).

Focus points

* Look for patterns when classifying your information, finding items with similar qualities.
* Slicing is an easy way to think about classifying your information, a vertical slice gives you the big picture while a horizontal slice gives you the detail on a topic or theme.
* Practise chunking information into bite-size portions so it is more manageable for your working memory.

* Memory network is a term used to represent a group of systems that allow a structured approach to storing and retrieving information.
* Some key memory networks include peg lists, method of loci and the major system.
* You can clean your memory networks by creating an eraser image.
* Use the rhyme list and number shape system to remember daily meetings.
* Get into the habit of creating memory networks, aim to build a new network once a week to begin with.
* Take advantage of Google Maps for a limitless source of memory networks.

Next steps

Your memory is only limited by your imagination. When you shift your focus away from memorizing and give your energy towards creating you realize that your potential is virtually limitless. While memorizing can sometimes feel a challenge, creating is just fun. What can you do in the next week that will start to channel your own ability to create?

7

The number system: Learn the value of remembering numbers

In this chapter you will learn:

▶ *the benefits of having a memory for numbers*

▶ *how to create a visual vocabulary for numbers*

▶ *temporary and permanent number systems*

▶ *when to use the right techniques for the right purpose*

▶ *how to set up a framework for statistics.*

What's in a number?

Key idea: The information age

Within the context of your career, remembering numbers could play a big role: for many it is an invaluable skill. This goes much further than showing off at parties or memorizing all the phone numbers in your contacts list; while impressive, in this day and age, most of this information is stored and easily accessible via your phone and backed up in 'the cloud'.

The real value in being able to remember numbers will vary for each individual depending on your career. If you have your own business, are involved in running projects or products, work in marketing, sales, law or perhaps politics, then the ability to pull key dates, figures and statistics out of your head is a very powerful technique. It demonstrates your knowledge and sets you up as a person of knowledge in your area, showing that you are up with the latest trends. Most likely it will also make you the go-to person and allow you to influence meetings and negotiations. If none of the above apply to you, there will be some key areas in your life where the ability to remember numbers will make a difference.

Remember this

Having worked as a product manager at the BBC, Microsoft and the *Telegraph* I have experienced first-hand benefit in being able to reel off the latest figures and statistics, not only for the product I was delivering but also for our competitors. For some, the value of being able to remember numbers and statistics is not always obvious. If this is the case, commit some time to discovering how this ability could add value in your own world.

Try it now: Numbers in your world

Time limit: 5 minutes

✳ Identify the key areas in your life where having the ability to memorize numbers would benefit you in some way, start with your personal life then think about your current job and finally move on to focusing on your future career. Imagine the skills you would need to achieve some of your future goals.

✳ Take five minutes to capture these thoughts.

A new vocabulary

The concept of making numbers memorable uses the same four core skills of creative memorization. In the same way that we use sound-images, natural-images and reference stories that refer to real-world information, for numbers we create a visual vocabulary of number-images that refer to a set of numbers.

RHYME LIST AND NUMBER SHAPE SYSTEM

Before looking at a more complex system, there are two very easy number systems that allow you to remember numbers. You are already familiar with these systems after working with them in the previous chapter – the rhyme list and the number shape system. Although their application is limited, they are a good introduction to the concept of creating a visual vocabulary for numbers.

Try it now: Remember your PINs

Time limit: 5 minutes

Steps

We will use visual embedding in this example.

Credit card PIN: 3801 – we use rhyme list and number shape system alternately, so 3801 would be Tree (3), Track (8), Hero (0), Pencil (1). Rather than create a narrative for this one you may use some simple visual embedding:

✳ Imagine you are in a room in your home. Your credit card is the same size as you. See it in every detail (use sense memory). Now on a table or the floor create the four images for each digit – again use sense memory to make them real.

✳ The credit card has four positions where you can embed these images; these will always follow the same order – on top, on the side, through the middle, on the bottom.

✳ Imagine the tree embedded in the top like a head, there are two tracks embedded in each side like arms, a hero is embedded in the middle like a belt, pencils are on the bottom like feet.

✳ Zoom into each image and use your sense memory to experience it in detail.

✳ Now take a step back and see the credit card with the tree, tracks, hero and pencils as one image.

✳ As you look at the image say 'Hi credit card, your number is 3801', then touch his head, shake his hand, straighten his belt and clean his shoes.

By doing the above you are engaging different neuronal pathways to remember one bit of information, which will make it much more likely to transfer it into long-term memory.

Ultimately we want to devise a visual vocabulary that will allow us to remember long sequences of numbers. The process of devising this visual vocabulary can be done in many different ways. While the rhyme system and number shape system could potentially fill this purpose, with anything over single digits they are not very practical.

Ideally we need an image for every two-digit number from 00 to 99: this way we can have the ability to remember a range of different number sequences.

You could attempt to do this through natural images, for example:

▶ The number 13 could be a **black cat**

▶ The number 18 is a **key**

▶ The number 88 is a **fat lady**

▶ The number 10 is the **prime minister**

▶ The number 64 is **Georgina the Giraffe** from 64 Zoo Lane

If you can think up 100 different images to represent all the numbers from 00 to 99, this is a pretty good place to start. However, it can be quite a challenging task.

Remember this

It is not necessary to have an elaborate system in order to create your number-images. The example above can be really useful for children and could as easily work for adults. When working with children, I create an image for each group of 10 (10 is Hen, 20 is Penguin, 30 is Snake); these are all arbitrary and worked out with whatever the children come up with. I then combine these images with the rhyme list, so 33 would be a Snake (30) wrapped around a Tree (3) – I usually introduce them to this system when learning times tables so there is a practical application for it.

THE MAJOR SYSTEM

The major system allows you to create a complete visual vocabulary for numbers. It uses a code in order to construct a number-image for each two-digit number from 00 to 99 (you can also use it to construct three- and four-digit numbers; we will focus on two here, though). There are several other systems out there that do the same thing in different ways: many people, especially memory athletes, have created their own systems to memorize thousands of consecutive digits in competition. Once you understand the concepts, you may find you want to create your own system.

Case study: World Memory Championships 732

When I began training for an hour-long memorization event it is fair to say that it was hard to know where to start and how to prepare. Ultimately I decided to jump in and give it a go. With 400 random digits in front of me, and an hour set on the timer I didn't know what to expect. Even though I knew the numbers systems and had put them into practice, this was a different league. After 30 minutes, I felt fairly drained, so stopped to see how much I could recall – all in all I was lucky to remember about 30 consecutive digits, I knew I had work to do.

There seemed like a few choices, I could do smaller sets of numbers and go for perfection OR try and build up some mental stamina while avoiding getting hung up on remember everything. I opted for the latter and employed some relativistic training. Simply put this is where you push yourself much further than you feel is possible and when you drop back to what feels comfortable you're further on than you were when you started.

In my case this meant training for an hour, aiming for 1,000 digits (more than I knew was possible at the time), going at speed, even if I didn't remember anything (which happened a number of times). Eventually your brain starts to catch-up and before long (the first four weeks) I was consistently doing 400 digits, at the end of three months I was doing between 600 and 1,000. So when it came to the World Memory Championships I was fairly confident I could achieve a decent score. I memorized 800 digits, however with a couple of mistakes this brought my score down to 732. Not bad for three months' training. The thing to take away here is that I had no special ability beforehand, just a great goal, a good strategy and a lot of perseverance. With those same ingredients anyone could do the same thing.

Remember this

In the 1995 World Memory Championships, I used the major system to remember those 732 consecutive digits in one hour. This was using the basic system: all in all I memorized about 400 images in the hour (each image represented two digits). Current memory athletes have more advanced systems than I used back then, allowing them to create an image that represents sometimes six digits rather than two. At the time of writing this book, the world record for most digits memorized in an hour is held by World Memory Champion Wang Feng with an astounding 2,660 digits.

For simplicity and understanding we will focus on the major system – as well as numbers, once you learn the major system it can come in very useful with creating mnemonic codes for other types of information which we will explore in Chapter 13 'Information overload'.

With enough practice you will be able to look at any number between 00 and 99 and instantly have an image to represent it.

► How it works

This major system has a code based on the principle that each number from 0 to 9 has a phonetic sound or sounds associated with it (we will refer to this as the major system code). From these sounds you can create words (images). The end result is that you build a vocabulary of images that represent numbers.

The following represents the phonetic sounds associated with each number from 0 to 9:

► 0 are the sounds that the letters Z and S make, as in Zorro and Snake

► 1 are the sounds that the letters T and D make, as in Teddy and Diamond

► 2 is the sound the letter N makes, as in Nuts

► 3 is the sound the letter M makes, as in Mike

► 4 is the sound the letter R makes, as in Rat

► 5 is the sound the letter L makes, as in Light

► 6 are the sounds the letters J, Sh and Ch make, as in Jam, Ship and Chips

► 7 are the sounds the letters K, G and NG make, as in Cat, Gun and riNG

► 8 are the sounds the letters F and V make, as in Fire and Van

► 9 are the sounds the letters P and B make, as in Pea and Bite

The sounds **A, E, I, O, U, W, H, Y** have no value. These no-value sounds enable us to create words.

It is important to note that it is **not the name** of the letter but the **sound of the letter** that equates to the number, so the word CeDaR would actually be the number 014, not 714, because the sound the C makes is S as in 'see'.

Example

► *22 could be NuN – N = 2, U has no value, N = 2*

► *37 could be MaC – M = 3, A has no value, C = 7*

► *59 could be LaB – L = 5, A has no value, B = 9*

Try it now: Learning the major system code

Time limit: 15 minutes

Use the following natural associations to remember the sounds associated with each number from 0 to 9. With repetition you will soon know these off by heart.

1   From a phonetic point of view, each group of sounds is created in the same part of the mouth.
    ✻ Z and S, for example, are made behind the teeth at the front of the mouth.
    ✻ T and D are made at the top and front of the mouth by the tongue.
    ✻ J, Sh and Ch are again made at the front of the mouth and form the same shape.
    ✻ K, G and NG are made by the tongue at the back of the mouth.
    ✻ F and V are made with the top teeth and bottom lip.
    ✻ P and B are made with the lips.

2   Spend a few minutes saying each group of sounds and notice where you make them in your mouth; by doing this the natural associations will make more sense for you.

3   Visualize the following natural associations and repeat them out loud, noticing the part of the mouth you are using. Run through this 5–10 times until you feel comfortable that you can recall the sound for each number.
    ✻ 0 starts with the sound Z
    ✻ 1 has 1 downstroke like T and D
    ✻ 2 has 2 downstrokes like N
    ✻ 3 looks like an M if you turn it on its side
    ✻ 4 – the last sound in four is R
    ✻ 5 digits on your hand; when you look at your palm with your thumb pointing to the side, it forms the letter L
    ✻ 6 flipped over resembles the letter J
    ✻ 7 stuck back to back forms the letter K
    ✻ 8 can look like a handwritten F
    ✻ 9 can look like a P or B

All of these associations will be temporary as after a short amount of time and practice you will just 'know' what sounds the numbers make.

Try it now: Find the number

Time limit: 5 minutes

Deconstruct this table of words into their correct numbers. Remember it is the sound the word makes that represents its number, not the letter, so a word such as 'mummy' would be 33, not 333; similarly a word such as 'cage' would be 76, not 77.

lab	duck	bin	fish	cape
mayor	roar	tail	can	phone
chief	shot	sail	net	leaf
beer	map	bash	nag	leach

▶ **The major system number matrix**

In the following table you can see an example of a number matrix created using the major system. Each of these images represents a number from 00 to 99. These are not the only images you could use. Using the major system, 65 could just as easily be Cello (sounds like 'chello') or Agile (sounds like 'ajile').

There is a learning curve in creating your own number matrix; however, if you have identified your purpose there is real value in it and therefore major benefits.

Major system number matrix example

00	01	02	03	04	05	06	07	08	09
Sauce	Sit	Sin	Sam	Soar	Sail	Sash	Sack	Safe	Zip
10	**11**	**12**	**13**	**14**	**15**	**16**	**17**	**18**	**19**
Daisy	Data	Dan	Dam	Door	Doll	Dash	Duck	Toffee	Tap
20	**21**	**22**	**23**	**24**	**25**	**26**	**27**	**28**	**29**
Noose	Net	Nun	Nam	Nero	Nail	Nash	Nag	Knife	Nappy
30	**31**	**32**	**33**	**34**	**35**	**36**	**37**	**38**	**39**
Mace	Mat	Minnie	Mummy	Marry	Mail	Mash	Mag	Mafia	Mop
40	**41**	**42**	**43**	**44**	**45**	**46**	**47**	**48**	**49**
Race	Rat	Rain	Rum	Roar	Rail	Rash	Rake	RAF	Rope
50	**51**	**52**	**53**	**54**	**55**	**56**	**57**	**58**	**59**
Lace	Lead	Alien	Lamb	Lara	Lilly	Lash	Lake	Leave	Lab
60	**61**	**62**	**63**	**64**	**65**	**66**	**67**	**68**	**69**
Jaws	Shot	Chain	Jam	Chair	Chilli	Gigi	Chuck	Chief	Chap
70	**71**	**72**	**73**	**74**	**75**	**76**	**77**	**78**	**79**
Case	Cat	Can	Gum	Car	Claw	Cash	Cake	Café	Cap

80	81	82	83	84	85	86	87	88	89
Vase	Fat	Vine	Foam	Fur	Fool	Fish	Fag	Viva	Phoebe

90	91	92	93	94	95	96	97	98	99
Boss	Bat	Bin	Beam	Beer	Bill	Bash	Bag	Beef	Poppy

Remember this

I find it extremely useful to create two images for each two-digit number. This is more advanced and utilized by many memory athletes. For each two-digit number, you can create a Person and an Object – for 49 I may have a Cowboy and a Rope, for 94 I may have Homer Simpson drinking beer. This allows me to combine the person from one number with the object of another – 4994 would be a Cowboy drinking Beer and 9449 would be Homer Simpson with a Rope. You can take this one step further and have a Person–Action–Object for each two-digit number: this takes some crafting and is probably only really useful if you intend to compete in memory competitions or are memorizing a lot of numbers in your career.

Try it now: Memorizing the number matrix (part 1)

Time limit: 30 minutes

* First construct your own number matrix using the major system.
* Create a table like the one above and write down words that make sense for you.
* Spend some time reading the words you have written and making sure you can decode them back into numbers.
* Get someone to give you one of the words you have written and tell them what the number is.

Try it now: Memorizing the number matrix (part 2)

Time limit: 30 minutes

In order to speed up the process of remembering your images, use a combination of a small memory network (10 nodes) and the chain method:
* Create a small memory network with 10 nodes (perhaps a simple journey).

* Use the chain method to memorize the images you have created for the numbers 00–09. This will allow you to refer to your number matrix without looking at the table you have created and create stronger synaptic connections.
* *Example – You are holding a giant bottle of sauce (00) while you sit (01) in a house of sin (02) with Sam (03) and soar (04) through space, powered by an atomic sail (05) made of a red satin sash (06) but you crash into a sack (07) and get locked in a safe (08) that is closed by a zip (09).*
* Do the same for each group, 20–29 and so on up to 90–99

The seven-day challenge

Over the next seven days spend ten minutes running through the matrix in your mind saying the numbers out loud as you see the images in your mind. Pay attention to any numbers you notice during your day and think how this would be represented as one of your images.

With practice the images that represent the numbers will become second nature; to be really effective you need to get to the stage where you no longer encode or decode the numbers and images; you just know that 24 is Nero or whatever image you choose to create. When this happens, remembering numbers is as easy as remembering a set of images.

Try it now: 100 digits
Time limit: 15 minutes

This exercise will help to familiarize you with your new number matrix. Feel free to refer to the number matrix you have written down, as you may not have memorized it yet.
* Create a memory network with 20 nodes (a journey with 20 locations).
* Memorize the following 40 digits by associating one image with a location.
9201982547 3847509377 5419152430 9607927152

Temporary or permanent

Depending on your purpose, the visual vocabulary you develop for your matrix may not fit every situation. At times when you have to memorize a number at high speed, the matrix of pre-determined images you create can be extremely beneficial. In some situations, especially when expanding your knowledge on a subject, it can be more beneficial to craft an image that is more closely associated with the information, as with a fact and a date:

▶ Emancipation of the Serfs, 1861

▶ Serfs being **FiSHeD** (861) out of Russia and set free.

▶ You usually have a good idea of which millennium it was in, so you need an image only for the last three digits.

You could therefore think of two types of system, each with a specific purpose: temporary numbers that utilize your numbers matrix and permanent numbers that are hand-crafted images using the phonetic code to create a word that is closely associated with the information being memorized. The latter takes slightly longer as you have the challenge of creating a unique word; however, it is more easily transferred into long-term memory and therefore requires less repetition.

Remember this

I like to use the matrix images I create specifically for either rapid memorization on the hoof, i.e. meeting room numbers, times, dates, statistics, etc., or mental workouts, demos, presentations and competitions. If, on the other hand, I wish to consolidate a number in my long-term memory, primarily general knowledge (history, entertainment, geography, etc.), anything with a fact and an associated date, I will generally construct a specific image using the major system code.

Try it now: Permanent numbers
Time limit: 15 minutes

Using the phonetic code, memorize the following inventions and the date they were invented using a specific image from the phonetic code:

Inventions	Reference story (examples)
Microscope – 1590	a microscope with huge red **LiPS**
Vacuum cleaner – 1901	vacuuming up **BiSTo** gravy granules
Pistol – 1540	a **LaRS** firing a pistol
Aeroplane – 1903	an aeroplane flying into a **BoSoM**
Inventions	**Reference story (your stories)**
Telescope – 1608	
Radar – 1904	
Glider – 1853	
Bicycle – 1861	
Electric battery – 1800	
Hot air balloon – 1709	

Remember this

There is a useful piece of software available called 2Know, from www. got2know.net/, that allows you to type in a number and it automatically generates a number of images based on the phonetic code, allowing you to choose the most appropriate one. Of course, you need to know your code extremely well to be able to translate images back to numbers at speed, but this will come with time and practice.

In practice

SET UP A FRAMEWORK FOR STATISTICS
Previously we looked at filing systems and the ability to classify and store your reference stories and link systems in a way that makes them easily accessible to you. To demonstrate the benefit of recalling numbers, let us look at a potential real-world situation for remembering statistics.

This framework will allow you to keep historical data for this fictitious company stored in your mind and allow you to update at weekly intervals with the option to store off-the-cuff data or day-to-day updates for key meetings or presentations.

▶ The fictitious company

MnemoBook – a large and successful social network site offering the ability to share and comment on the latest to do with brain research, memory improvement and personal development. MnemoBook have embedded social functionality allowing people to share their content.

▶ KPIs (Key Performance Indicators)

The statistics they are capturing are:

▶ Numbers of shares per week

▶ Number of comments on those shares per week

Here is an example of some historical statistics over a four-week period:

21/03–27/03 Content shared: 23,576 – up 117%

Comments per share: 9 – up 19%

28/03–03/04 Content shared: 65,604 – up 178%

Comments per share: 9 – down 4.4%

04/04–10/04 Content shared: 89,054 – up 36%

Comments per share: 10 – up 8.1%

11/04–17/04 Content shared: 76,571 – down 14%

Comments per share: 6 – down 33%

▶ The memory network

For this example you could construct a combination of the journey method and item system. There are 52 weeks in a year so 52 locations give you the ability to store a year's worth of data. Over time this will give you the ability to report on percentage increases month by month and per quarter, giving you different ways to report on the data.

Since you will be accumulating this data over a long period of time, it is not essential to create all 52 locations; you could start with four, allowing you to capture the past four weeks. If this were real, you would most likely create another four so you were prepared for the month ahead.

Let us imagine that there are four locations for four weeks: you will allocate the name of the month to each location and the date will be a number-image associated with the centre of that location. Each location will have four items (these are your nodes).

Example (you can make up your own nodes for the last three locations):

▶ *Coffee shop (March), number-image: NeT (21)*

▶ *Coffee machine, content shared: NaM (23), LuGGaGe (576) – Nam drinking coffee with his luggage*

▶ *Cake stand, up by: TooTHaCHe (117) – a cake with toothache*

▶ *Sofa, comments per share: SoaP (09) – a sofa covered in soap*

▶ *Chair: up by: DeBBie (19) – a chair with Debbie Reynolds dancing on it*

▶ *Marks and Spencer (March), number-image: NaVy (28)*

▶ *W.H. Smith (April), number-image: SoaR (04)*

▶ *Boots (April), number-image: DaTa (11)*

From the above we can see that the coffee shop represents 21 March. Content shared is 23,576, up by 117%, and comments per share are 9, up by 19%.

Try it now: Memorizing statistics

Time limit: 30 minutes

Create your own nodes for each location.
Memorize the rest of the statistics.

Information	Reference story (your stories)
28/3	
65,604 – up 178%	
9 – down 4.4%	
4/4	
89,054 – up 36%	
10 – up 8.1%	
11/4	
76,571 – down 14%	
6 – down 33%	

Test it

* In w/c 28/3 was content shared up or down and by how much?
* In w/c 11/4 what was the amount of content shared, was this up or down on previous weeks?
* In what week was content shared at its highest?
* In w/c 4/4 what was the average comments per share?

Of course as the stats go up or down each week there will be a reason, a story that goes along with it; you can easily capture this story within your locations. For example, stats went down w/c 11/4 because the application that measures the statistics went offline for one day that week – you could imagine the application falling over, attached to a particular item in your location to represent this. Ultimately, the insight behind the statistics is the thing that is really important, as this will give you knowledge about what is working and what is not.

Remember this

Although you used only four nodes per location here, in a real-world situation I would suggest creating around ten nodes. The good thing is that you don't have to create that many in advance.

Focus points

* Identify the areas in your life where being able to remember numbers will add some value.
* To memorize numbers, create a visual vocabulary by constructing a set of number-images.
* Learn the major system code in order to turn any number into a memorable number-image.
* Allocate time to design your own number matrix for the numbers 00 to 99.
* Take the seven-day challenge and spend ten minutes a day mastering your number matrix.
* Practise hand-crafting permanent numbers for specific information.

Next steps

By having confidence in remembering numbers, dates and statistics it can empower you to bring details to conversations, build credibility and influence with data. Whether you work with numbers day to day or not, having this skill can set you apart in your career and your business.

Memorize a simple statistic and use it within a conversation at some point in the next 24 hours. This could be a conversation with a colleague, a friend, your partner or if you have them your kids!

8

Mind mapping: Create, capture, consume and communicate

In this chapter you will learn:

- ▶ *how mind maps reflect the way we think*
- ▶ *how to find your own style and own your mind maps*
- ▶ *step by step how to mind map*
- ▶ *to use mind maps to create, capture, consume and communicate.*

Mind maps are creative tools that allow a person to create, capture, consume and communicate. Although visual thinking has been around for thousands of years, Tony Buzan is the originator of mind maps.

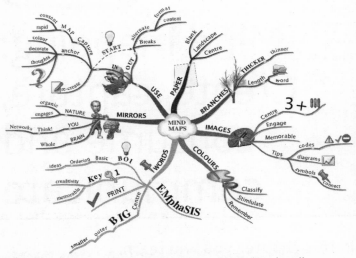

Figure 8.1 A mind map (created using ThinkBuzan'siMindMap http://www.thinkbuzan.com).

Mirror the mind

Key idea: Mind maps

One of the core ideas behind mind mapping is that it mirrors the way we think. In the same way that our brain is constantly forming connections and pathways, mind maps capture and reflect some of those key associations we make in our mind.

On the surface, mind mapping can appear a simple process that produces an interesting way of capturing notes. Once you delve deeper into the mechanics of mind mapping, you start to see there are subtle complexities that can play a significant role in their effectiveness.

If you have used mind maps in the past, you may have had the same reaction that many people seem to have to Marmite – you love it or you hate it – 'you just get it' or 'it's just not how your mind works'. Both are valid perceptions. The main difference that a mind map has is that it capitalizes on more sensory inputs and therefore facilitates more opportunities to make connections to the information, whether you are brainstorming, taking notes in a meeting, learning information from a book or communicating your ideas to others.

Case study: Mind map as a study technique

Farrand, P., Hussain, F. and Hennessy, E. (2002) 'The efficacy of the "mind map" study technique.', *Medical education.*, 5(36).

In a 2002 study fifty second- and third-year medical students were asked to complete a short test on a 600-word passage before splitting into two groups. The first used 'self-selected study technique' the second received training in 'mind mapping'. Both groups were shown the passage of text again and asked to use their study technique.

Recall of the groups were tested after an interference task and again one week later. After a week the mind map group showed a 10 per cent improvement in factual knowledge than the self-selected study group. However motivation for using mind maps again was lower in the mind map group.

Remember this

I have been employing mind maps since the early 1990s. From my experience of working with many people over the years, those who say 'it's not how I work' have either misunderstood what a mind map is and usually produce something similar to a spider-gram or have got confused by 'rules'. My suggestion if yours was the latter experience is to wipe the slate clean and explore the ideas in this chapter as if you were seeing them for the first time, holding back any preconceived ideas and enjoying playing with the 'Try it nows'. Mind maps do require reconditioning of how you 'operate'; after all, most of us have been conditioned to write linear notes and create lists from an early age (they still have their use, by the way).

This can have an impact on a person's motivation when they first start putting mind maps into practice. It can 'feel' harder than writing a list. The key in the beginning is finding ways to use mind maps that give you instant value and rewards – creating new ideas or mapping out problems and solutions can be a great place to start.

MIND MAPPING AND THE LEARNING CYCLE

Mind mapping naturally employs the learning cycle. As mentioned, it has many sensory inputs, allows you to reflect on the big picture and the details, creates an opportunity to abstract your own thoughts and take action through adding new branches, through rehearsal or through putting the information to use. The outcome of this is that your brain makes more connections to the information, which in turn makes the information more memorable.

If you used a mind map to learn a speech or presentation, once the message, outcomes, ideas and structure are in place, you complete the circle by putting it into action.

Act out! using the map as a prompt (we will go into detail on this in the section *The four Cs* below).

Try it now: Your current process

Time limit: 10 minutes

Before you begin, get either a notepad or paper and a pen.

Think back to a time (it can be recently) when you had to capture or consume some information: perhaps you were studying for an exam, taking notes in a meeting or learning new skills for work. As you remember this situation, write down:

- How did you capture your notes?
- How did you memorize these notes?
- How did you revise or review the information?
- How hard or easy was it to remember the information on a scale of 0–10?

❋ How long did you retain the information for?
❋ How have you captured the answer to these questions?
As you review what you have written, circle which of the following skills
you believe you have put into practice:

Left brain dominant	Right brain dominant
Logic	Colour
Linearity	Dimension
Lists	Daydreaming
Sequence	Rhythm
Words	Imagination
Analysis	Gestalt (whole picture)
Numbers	Spatial awareness

Mind mapping, rather than using one set of skills more than
another, incorporates all of these skills: words with colour, logic
with imagination, sequence with rhythm, detail with the big
picture.

Remember this

When I first thought about this, I remembered note-taking at school
(back in the 1970s/80s) and noticed that I scored high on the more
dominant left-brain skills – logic, lists, sequence, words – and I would
use repetition to drill it into my head. However, I hardly had anything on
imagery, dimension, daydreaming (I would daydream but it wouldn't be
connected to the stuff I was learning). My notes were, for the most part,
black and white, nearly all in list format, sometimes pictures or diagrams,
but they were never connected and I had no way of seeing the big
picture. I could cram for exams but nothing 'stuck'.

In this sense, you could think of mind mapping as a whole-brain tool.
Mind maps mirror the learning cycle and trigger activity throughout the
brain, facilitating more connections.

Mind maps and you

Try it now: What's your style?
Time limit: 3 minutes

* Imagine that you are going into an interview situation or a meeting where you have to tell someone all about yourself: background, qualities, strengths, weaknesses, likes, loves, goals, etc. Thinking about involving as many of the skills we have previously mentioned as possible, spend just three minutes creating what you believe to be a mind map to reflect this information.

* *Note: There is no right or wrong answer here, the purpose of this action is merely to get you to start thinking about incorporating different cortical skills and finding your natural style.*

Remember this

Visual note-taking is also a popular method of visual thinking; it has many similar qualities to mind mapping. I would liken it more to the chain method as it takes you on a journey. Since my focus has been in the mind mapping arena, I don't go into detail around visual note-taking here, but there are some excellent resources available on the internet if you want to explore this further.

How to mind map

You don't have to be an artist to mind map or do visual note-taking. If you follow some simple guidelines, your mind maps will be extremely effective whether you wish to create, capture, consume or communicate.

Try it now: The story of a mind map
Time limit: 15 minutes

Here are the steps to creating a mind map. As you read through the following, reflect back to the mind map picture at the beginning of the chapter, thinking about how you could create your own. We will assume you are mind mapping by hand.

Paper
* Whenever possible use 'blank' A3, A4 or A5 paper or whiteboard (avoid using lined paper as this imposes a linear structure).
* Use landscape orientation.
* Always start with a central image.

Branches
* Branches give the mind map its style; this is a big factor in a mind map catching your 'attention' and 'engaging' you.
* Be as creative as you like with what your branches look like; if you are creating a mind map to reflect music, then each branch could be an instrument.
* Work to give your mind map an organic look and feel as if it is a living organism, radiating and connecting, helping to bring information to life and therefore make it more memorable.
* The branch you use should only be as long as the word or image it supports; this allows those words and images to be closely connected, when you recall those words they will be associated spatially.
* The branches should avoid being linear; think of flowing movements or even use imagery to represent your branches.
* Connectors are branches that connect 'other' branches together; there are no hard and fast rules, however, it is recommended that the branches are in close vicinity, otherwise your mind map can quickly turn into spaghetti junction. If you do use a connector that traverses your mind map, do so sparingly.

Images
* Imagery lies at the heart of your mind map.
* Always start with the central image; if it is text then make it 3D.
* Give your central image at least three colours (if you are capturing at high speed, this may not be possible).
* Images should be used across your map to make information memorable and stand out, or sum up a complex idea in one picture; the old adage 'A picture speaks a thousand words' is especially true with a mind map.
* Think of codes as images that tell you something about the word on the branch; it may draw special attention to it or give the word a higher priority.

* Symbols are similar to codes, but they differ in their purpose: whereas codes give specific meaning to a branch, symbols tell the story of relationships between branches.
  ▷ There is a **Pin** on the **Symbols branch** and on the **Words branch** – this implies that 'symbols' **connect** 'words'.
  ▷ The light bulb on the branch **BOI** (Basic Ordering Ideas – these are the words on your Level 1 Branches – PAPER, BRANCHES, IMAGES, COLOURS, WORDS, MIRRORS, USE) also appears on the connector line **Start** – the relationship here is that whenever we USE a mind map to take information in or get information out we should start with **BOI** wherever possible
* Diagrams and charts are used in many situations, by bringing your Powerpoint chart into a mind map you can show where it connects to the Big Picture (this is especially useful with mind map software).
* Over time you will start to build your own vocabulary for codes and symbols, a common language that will help you create quicker and stronger connections with new information.

Colours

* Use colours to classify the information and ideas on your mind map (you may use colour already to do this – colour-coding sections of a folder or using highlighters to make specific points stand out). This helps identify structures within the map. Colour is a simple way of attracting attention to information with similar qualities.
* There are usually emotional connections to colour (blue feels cool or cold, yellow feels warm and sunny, etc.); this can help to stimulate your imagination and inspire imagery.
* There are some great books that demonstrate the difference colour makes with regard to how much you can remember. *The Human Brain Colouring Book* is a good example of this. You participate in the learning process: by colouring in you have to reflect on the information and make more connections to it; you will abstract your own thoughts and put them into action. Colour not only makes your information stand out, it makes it memorable.

Words

* Words should be BIGGER in the centre and smaller as the branches spread out.
* Use different SiZes to emphasize words.

* Only one word per branch; efficiency with words will make your mind maps easier to remember and give you freedom to be more creative as concepts are broken down and separated onto different branches.
  ▷ One word per branch will save space, allowing you to capture and consume more information.
  ▷ Probably the most challenging part about constructing mind maps is condensing your thoughts down to single words: the temptation is to write short phrases or sentences across your branches. While this may be useful in pulling out quotes for presentations, you should practise using minimal words. This will also benefit you if you pull the words onto a memory network.
* When reviewing your mind map you should practise seeing the key word and reciting the concepts, ideas and thoughts behind it.

Mirrors
* Nature – has an organic look and feel that attracts attention and engages in the information (it still has to be defined otherwise the map can become undecipherable, a common reason why mind maps can confuse).
* You – it reflects how we naturally think through imagination and association, mirroring the networks in our mind.
* A whole brain tool involving many cortical skills.

Use
Mind maps have two channels, taking in and putting out:

* Taking in
  ▷ Capture the information (potentially rapidly).

  ▷ Anchor the information by colouring, decorating, adding in branches for your own thoughts and questions.

  ▷ Afterwards recreate your map to consolidate the information.

* Putting out
  ▷ Alternate the content (branches, connectors and words) with the format (colours, images, codes and symbols).

  ▷ Take regular breaks.

Remember this

As a kid I think it is fair to say that I felt I was good at art. After leaving school and not drawing for ten years I seemed to lose the ability. When I first started mind mapping, I also had some beliefs about what people would think if my drawings looked childish. What I found was the opposite: people are usually intrigued when you mind map (especially in a meeting situation). Since I have been mind mapping for years now, the 'quality' of the maps has improved and I enjoy drawing again.

Try it now: Your mind map
Time limit: 15 minutes

Now recreate the mind map above using the style that feels right, adding in colour and any images that come to mind – it does not have to look like the mind map above but it should contain the same branches and words. Add at least two more branches, one that captures what you feel the benefits are, one that captures the challenges and any others that come to mind.

Remember this

Do not be afraid of making mistakes. One thing I have noticed, especially when working with groups or individuals, is that people think it has to be perfect or as close as possible. The purpose is not to create a work of art, it is to either get something inside your head so you can use it or help to get something out of your head to solve problems, develop ideas or communicate messages. Our instinct can be that we are creating 'a picture' so we do not want to make mistakes; avoid falling into this trap. If it helps, buy a small whiteboard, where if something is not right, you can just rub it out and start again. I always have two spare branches on my mind maps to capture things that 'crop up' such as random thoughts and questions.

The four Cs

We have explored ideas behind mind mapping, how mind maps could work for you and how to mind map. The four Cs cover the main areas where mind mapping can be applied: create, capture, consume and communicate.

Although they are represented here as four separate entities, they most often cross over so that a mind map that starts for the purpose of capturing information in a meeting quickly becomes one that helps you consume and remember, communicate back what has been said and create new possibilities or solutions.

In the age of iPads and similar devices, software mind maps have made a big leap. They make it relatively quick to move your thoughts around, edit, add colour, link to documents or references on the internet and create a set of minutes or report on the outcomes of the meeting.

Paper and pen can still be quicker although there are disadvantages when capturing information: you generally don't have too much time to swap colours, although not a big drawback as afterwards you can add colour and imagery to create strong connections with information that is of importance.

Since you now understand 'how to mind map', there are a few subtleties to think about when putting them into practice.

Remember this

My preference for capturing in meetings is a simple A5 whiteboard, with a coloured pen and an eraser. I remember when I had my first meeting with the new general manager taking over one of the departments at the BBC. iPads were very popular and this quickly became a topic of conversation; he even took a photograph. I later joked that he'd sent it round to Microsoft with the caption, 'This is how they do things at the Beeb.' This experience happened at pretty much every meeting I went to. The upshot is, you tend to be remembered.

CREATE

The benefits of mind mapping in the area of creation are many: whether it's a brainstorming new ideas session, solving a problem or creating a presentation, a mind map can help give you quality results.

▶ State

Make sure you get yourself into a creative state. Think back to the chapter on creative memorization where we talked about sense memory and emotional recall.

▶ Think about your purpose and your ideal outcome.

▶ Use active daydreaming and draw words and pictures that represent this ideal outcome.

▶ Questions

The questions you ask yourself and the self-talk that happens in your mind will direct and guide your output. In simple terms, ask a negative question, 'why can't I think of anything?' and your brain will go in search of an answer; at some point it will come back with one – you don't know enough, you're not creative, you're not good at this stuff.

Ask yourself a different question with the 'expectation' of getting an answer and you will get some useful feedback. What happens next? What would make the biggest difference? How can I make this work? Questions such as these asked in a curious and expectant way will create motivation and send your brain on a quest for knowledge. As you think up good questions to ask, add them to your mind map.

▶ Overcoming blocks

At some point you will have a mental block or just need time to reflect, gather your thoughts and decide what happens next. When this happens, let yourself focus on the format of your map, creating imagery around certain areas of interest, colouring and doodling, using codes and symbols to highlight words or build relationships.

While you are in this state, you will notice that ideas will come to you for new content and connections with branches.

Alternate back and forth between the content of your map and the format; this will feed a rhythm that will allow you to progress with your ideas.

CAPTURE

In whatever career you are in, for most there will be occasions (sometimes frequent) when you have to capture notes, facts and actions, whether it is in meetings, presentations, conferences, seminars, lectures or classes.

▶ What's relevant?

The key is to capture the information that is 'relevant': while this seems an obvious statement, it can be a challenge. Since you have to hone your thoughts down to single words, mind mapping conditions you in this art.

While listening and watching presentations, try to limit what you capture to information that you feel or think is connected to the purpose. Do not capture every little detail. If you are not sure, add a word to your question or thought branch that you can come back to later. This takes some practice; with enough repetition you will soon learn to 'filter' most of what is important.

▶ Templates

Start with a template where possible, at minimum this is a central image (representing the topic), a branch for ideal outcomes, thoughts and questions and branches for any known agenda.

▶ Time-sensitive

When capturing information there is less time to reflect, so you are relying on a clear purpose to guide you to what is relevant. Pragmatically you often won't have time to swap colours or draw lots of pictures, so if capturing at high speed, build the skeleton of your map that you can add to later to anchor the concepts and ideas in your mind.

CONSUME

Whereas capture is about identifying what is relevant, making connections and organizing, consuming is about understanding and remembering the information on your maps so you can put it into practice.

Mind maps 'map' perfectly to the learning cycle, taking information you have created or captured and making sense of it, through reflection, abstraction and some form of action. Comprehension starts when you are capturing and continues as you consume; depending on the complexity of the information you can allocate more time to this process, creating stronger connections with the information.

▶ Input

With so much information to remember being passed around and the importance of keeping your knowledge (especially in your chosen field) up to date, it is useful if not imperative to have a way of consuming that information and having a reference for a later date.

You can make mind maps part of how you operate: as they are naturally more memorable than linear notes, they can be used to consume information from books, emails, documents and research in preparation for future meetings, presentations or interviews.

Used in conjunction with creative memorization, you have a powerful mental toolkit at your disposal.

▶ Reflect

To understand the information you have captured, run through the map, reflecting on what it means. How does it relate to things you already know? What is this new information similar to? You are aiming to make some form of connection to help with your understanding. Metaphors are useful for this. Earlier we used the metaphor about the brain having over 100 billion neurons and compared that to the 100 billion trees in the rainforest; this was an easy picture to reflect on that gave an understanding to something which may have been completely new.

▶ Abstract

When you have a difficult topic to grasp, abstracting your ideas helps you to take ownership. You then have to ask questions that will lead you towards a solution, in the same way as you would if you were creating a solution (which effectively you are). One of those solutions might be to ask someone for help or clarification. Abstracting is about taking what you have learned and putting it into your own words, making your own connections and points of reference to the information.

▶ Actions

Decide what form of action you need to take if any: this may simply be storing the map for reference. If this is the case, you should start to build a classification for it or add it to one that already exists so it can be useful to you in the future. Perhaps you need it for a specific meeting or to gain knowledge that will help you perform more efficiently in your role.

The actions you take will be linked to your purpose: if you are mind mapping a presentation, you should rehearse using the mind map as a prompt, standing up and speaking aloud. If you are memorizing for an exam, you should test yourself by answering questions, initially using the mind map as a prompt and then without (mixed with creative memorization this becomes highly effective). If you have mapped notes from a meeting, simply play them back at the end of the meeting as a summary.

The actions you take complete the learning cycle and give you more sensory input to process, strengthening your connections to the information.

Case study: Executive coaching

During my time at the BBC I was lucky enough to be trained as an executive coach. While I had worked as a coach for a number of years picking up various strategies along the way, it seemed hugely valuable to go through a more structured programme that I could bring into my own coaching work.

Throughout the course of a year we covered a vast array of skills and strategies as well as practical work with clients; over this time I was able to employ a number of memory strategies as well as create a few more (creative listening being one of them).

At the end of the programme there was an opportunity to create a mind map that captured the essence of what I had taken away. For this, I took the approach of using Edward De Bono's Six Thinking Hats, a process for parallel thinking. Each coloured hat representing a different function:

* White – information
* Red – feelings and emotion
* Black – risks and judgement
* Yellow – optimism and value
* Green – creativity and possibilities
* Blue – control and outcomes.

Combining De Bono's thinking hats metaphor with a mind map facilitated the consolidation of over a year worth of study and practice into one sheet of A3. Behind each word or picture were a number of stories and memories. This mind map had become a snapshot into a magnificent set of experiences.

Figure 8.2 (Hand-drawn mind map created by Mark Channon)

COMMUNICATE

Mind maps can be powerful tools for presentation and collaboration. Your aim should be to utilize the learning cycle in order to give your group or individual the best experience, to have them understand your message and give them something they can take away and use.

▶ Groups

Because of the artistic and organic look and feel of a mind map, it naturally catches your attention. While looking at a mind map, it should tease curiosity within a group.

As with all presentations it is important that 'you' tell the story, the mind map is there as a visual reference that helps make your message more memorable. While you are giving a presentation, individuals will have their own stories and connections happening inside their heads; by focusing on specific parts of the mind map at the right time, the stories in their heads will become connected to your mind map.

Example

Imagine you are looking at a picture of the cortical skills of the brain on a mind map. I start talking about the time I was at school with a particular teacher who was quite strict (you may have had a teacher like this at your own school), wouldn't stand for any day dreaming nonsense and woe betide if you spoke out of turn, everything had to be written out neatly in black pen and this meant the children in that class were using primarily left-brain skills.

Chances are this may have triggered a memory of when you were at school. Since you are looking at the image of the cortical skills and you have experience of what that means, your experience gets associated with the picture on my mind map.

While or after the group reflect on their own experiences you should be challenging them to search for their own interpretations or solutions. This can be as simple as facilitating questions.

This should all build towards the group taking some form of action, making the information you have imparted to them useful to them in some way.

With a computer mind map presentation, you can capture their questions and thoughts live on the appropriate branch; if it's a large group, you may want someone to add these to the map while you continue to engage the audience.

▶ One to one

If you are one-to-one with someone, mind maps are a subtle yet powerful tool. Without even actively saying anything, people will be drawn to the map, which you can use to reflect what has been said and build on ideas. It is therefore a great tool for helping to build rapport.

If you do mind map on a one-to-one basis, make sure you only capture the essential details. It is important to be connected to the person you are speaking to and use the map sparingly.

If you get the balance right, one-to-ones are a great opportunity to have some real collaboration and engage some physicality in the creation of the mind map. Depending on your level of rapport, you can ask the person you are working with to add branches and draw pictures to explain what they mean, then reflect and summarize that back to them.

The mind map becomes a shared experience.

In practice

We have only scratched the surface of mind mapping and there is a lot more underneath; ultimately it is about finding your own style and putting it into practice.

Try it now: Where in your life?
Time limit: 15 minutes

Think of all the different areas in your life where you could apply mind mapping. Create a mind map with these branches as a minimum:

* Create
* Capture
* Consume
* Communicate
* Thoughts
* Questions

On each branch connect areas of your life where you could put these skills into practice.

Focus points

* Mind maps are tools for creating, capturing, consuming and communicating.
* Mind maps mirror the way we think, reflecting the internal connections in your mind.
* Identify the level of cortical skills you use in your current note-taking; compare this with how many you use when mind mapping or when using visual notes.
* Find your style – think about what you can do to make mind maps work for you.
* Regularly practise mind mapping following the *How to mind map* guidelines, using branches, images, colours and words.
* Create with your mind maps by getting in the right state, using the power of questions to guide you and overcoming blocks by alternating format and content.
* Capture effectively with your mind maps by priming yourself for relevant information, setting up templates and being pragmatic about what you can achieve in the time you have.
* Consume rapidly through incorporating an abundance of sensory input, using your map as a mirror to reflect on what you know, abstracting and capturing your own thoughts and questions and using your map as a tool to take some form of action.
* Communicate dynamically with groups using your mind map to raise curiosity and 'tell the story'. Engage deeply on a one-to-one level in a subtle and rapport-building way that evokes collaboration.
* Mind maps can be used for facilitating ideas, problem solving, increasing comprehension, improving memory retention, rapid note taking, engaging presentations and more.

Next steps

For the beginner mind maps can take some growing into, once a person gets the idea of mind mapping into their body though, not only can it open up a more effective way of learning and communicating, it can be a fun way of focusing your mind around new ideas and opportunities.

Start putting mind maps to work for you, remember, it doesn't have to be perfect – jump in, give it a go, find your style and experiment with what works well for you.

9

Reading strategies: Double or triple your speed

In this chapter you will learn:

▶ *how to measure your current reading speed*

▶ *benefits of creating purpose and direction*

▶ *how to capture the 10,000-foot view*

▶ *how to double your reading speed with speed reading.*

There are many books that go into great detail on reading strategies. The purpose of this section is to give you practical techniques you can start using today that will speed up consumption and comprehension of reading material.

Benchmark

If you want to increase your reading speed, it is a valuable use of time to benchmark yourself so you can measure your success as your speed increases. This will also help create beliefs to back up your progress and let you identify which areas you need to improve in.

 Try it now: Benchmark your speed
Time limit: 5 minutes

Before beginning, choose a book that is of interest to you and find yourself a stopwatch.
* Note where you begin and, when you are ready, start reading.
* After one minute, stop reading and make a note of where you got to.
* Count the number of **lines** you have read in total and make a note.
* Count the number of **words** in three lines and divide by 3 (this gives an average).
* Average **number of words x number of lines** = words per minute (**wpm**).
If there is an average of 12 words per line and you have read 50 lines, that would give you a benchmark reading speed of 600 wpm.

Purpose and direction

When you think back to books or documents you have read in the past, how much attention have you paid before you start reading to your ultimate purpose? Do you generally have a good idea of what you are looking for? Are you priming yourself for information that is relevant?

As we have previously seen, priming is an important aspect of setting ourselves up to remember. By having a strong purpose and direction about why this information is important and what you think is relevant inside this book or document, you set your brain's radar to be on the lookout.

Try it now: Finding purpose and direction

Time limit: 3 minutes

* Think of a problem or challenge that needs to be solved.
* What do you gain by solving it; what is your purpose?
* Choose a factual book that you think has some information that could help.
* Reaffirm your purpose.
* By simply reading the table of contents, identify whether this book is relevant. If it isn't, move on.
* What level of detail do you need to understand?
* How much time do you think you will need to commit?

Example

* *Imagine you are a manager and have a problem with team performance.*
* *Your purpose is to find some way to identify the issues and improve team performance (your purpose is now clear – you are primed).*
* *You go in search of books that could help and select Ken Blanchard's* One Minute Manager *book about building high performing teams.*
* *You reaffirm your purpose.*
* *You scan the index and identify anything that looks relevant, e.g. techniques you could put into practice straight away and measure against current performance. This book has things that look relevant so you continue.*
* *The level of detail you need will be high around the one or two techniques you identify and can be less for the rest of the book.*
* *Taking the size of the book into account, you could estimate that within two hours you will have identified what you need and have understood it to a level where you could put it into practice and test it out.*

10,000-foot view

Once your purpose has been established, you can use previewing as a technique to set up the mental scaffolding to give you the 10,000-foot view. Previewing should be a fairly short phase lasting no longer than two to five minutes: explore and seek out parts of the book that catch your attention in line with your purpose. Reflect on parts of the book that are familiar to you and dive briefly into any sections that have new information. There is no need to stop for more than three to five seconds.

You may find that something is so interesting that you just start reading: avoid this trap; the main objective for previewing is to build up a big picture view and identify some nuggets of interest.

After previewing, it is useful to consolidate your thoughts, running the learning cycle, reflecting, abstracting and creating some new actions. If mind maps are working for you, it is a great opportunity to put them into practice. Without going back to the book for any more detail, you simply start mind mapping what you can remember from your preview. You will be tempted to look at the book for details: avoid this and just create a branch that captures questions you have or things you can't quite remember but want to dig into in more detail. Add a branch that communicates how you would put some of the information into practice. While reflecting on the mind map as a whole you can also clarify your purpose.

 Try it now: Preview time
Time limit: 10 minutes

Find a book of your choice and spend no longer than five minutes previewing and five minutes mind mapping your thoughts.

Double your speed

Speed reading strategies deal with some common reading problems, e.g. back-skipping, when you read a sentence and then unconsciously skip back to read it again, and regression, when you go back to words, phrases or sentences you didn't understand or think you need to clarify.

The following strategies offer the opportunity to at least double your current reading speed.

GUIDING

As children you would have been taught to read by using your finger, guiding your eye across the page. When reading, your eye moves in fixations, rather than a smooth movement: it will jump across points in a sentence. Someone practised in speed reading will take larger jumps, pause for less time at each jump, avoid jumping backwards and take in more words with each jump. The outcome of this is that reading speed is increased and comprehension is increased as more words are taken in together.

Try it now: Chopsticks!
Time limit: 5 minutes

Continue with the book you chose for the first 'Try it now' of this chapter and get your stopwatch ready. Find yourself a pen or some type of pointer; a chopstick works very well. Use your chopstick as a guide, in the same way you used your finger as a child; move the chopstick underneath the sentence, let your eyes take in groups of words at a time. As you move the chopstick smoothly from line to line, do not back-skip or regress to things you have previously read.

For this test, move the pointer slightly faster than is comfortable.

* Note where you begin and, when you are ready, start reading.
* After one minute stop reading and make a note of where you got to.
* Count the number of lines you have read in total and make a note.
* Count the number of words in three lines and divide by 3 to give you an average.
* Average number of words x number of lines = words per minute (wpm).
* Compare this wpm with your previous wpm.

PERIPHERAL

This is a technique that is referred to in Ron Davis's *The Gift of Dyslexia* that focuses on the mind's eye – 'a mental perception point at which a person looks at mental images or thoughts'. The mind's eye is mentioned in various reading books, yoga classes and martial arts; this is so you become more aware of the world around you – in martial arts this makes you more effective when blocking attacks.

Try it now: Engage your peripheral
Time limit: 2 minutes

By engaging your peripheral vision, your scope of vision widens and also deepens. There are several ways to practise this that have been referred to in many books. A good one is in Paul Scheele's *Photoreading*, where he refers to this as the 'tangerine technique', although it could be any object you wish, a tennis ball or any small object.

* Imagine that there is a tennis ball or tangerine in front of you; see it in every detail (think back to the sense memory exercise).
* Now reach forward and pick it up; examine it.
* Now place it at the back of your head (on top of your crown).
* As you let go, become aware that it is still there.
* As you focus on it, notice that it drifts back about 15 cms (6 inches), upwards at 45 degrees.
* Imagine that you are now 'seeing from this point' – your mind's eye.
* See the page in front of you from this point.

This will feel strange to begin with and take some practice, but you should notice your field of vision opening up.

SUBVOCALIZATION

Part of the objective of speed reading is not to subvocalize, i.e. say every word in your head while reading. Having said that, it can be very effective to vocalize particular words that spring out and catch your attention: these tend to be the ones that are of most relevance.

Try it now: Silent reading
Time limit: 5 minutes

Bring the last few 'activities' together. Use a pointer, find your mind's eye and read the next section without subvocalizing. Again, move the pointer faster than is comfortable

* Note where you begin and, when you are ready, start reading.
* After one minute stop reading and make a note of where you got to.
* Count the number of lines you have read in total and make a note.

* Count the number of words in three lines and divide by 3 to give you an average.
* Average number of words x number of lines = words per minute (wpm).
* Compare this wpm with your previous wpm.

Key idea: Believe you can

Belief can have a big impact on performance, whether it is a belief about what we can remember, how good we are at sports or how fast we can read. By imagining yourself going faster or performing better than you thought was possible, you create positive references that support beliefs about what is possible.

Try it now: How far can you go?

Time limit: 5 minutes

* Stand up straight and, keeping your feet still throughout, raise your right arm directly in front of you, pointing your finger straight ahead.
* Now, moving around to your right, go as far as you can and note where your finger is pointing.
* Bring your arm back to resting.

Now we condition a belief.

* Imagine that you are standing up as you were before, right arm raised directly in front of you, pointing your finger straight ahead.
* Imagine moving around to your right, but this time you notice that you go much further than you did before and the movement seems effortless; notice how this feels; see how much further you have gone than you did previously.
* Open your eyes, stand up, raise your right arm directly in front of you and go as far as you can round to the right.

After doing this, a large number of people will go at least six inches further than they did the first time. You can use this same technique with reading. Imagine yourself reading faster than you ever have before, effortlessly gliding across sentences, capturing whole sentences at a time, instantly making sense of everything you read. If you make this real enough in your mind, your brain will start creating references that this is possible.

Try it now: Speed reading in action

Time limit: 5 minutes

Bring together all the reading strategies in this section. Spend the first two minutes imagining yourself reading faster than ever before, set your mind's eye, get your pointer ready, only subvocalize essential words and push yourself faster than before, gliding your pointer across the page, taking in groups of words with each jump.

※ Note where you begin and, when you are ready, start reading.
※ After one minute stop reading and make a note of where you got to.
※ Count the number of lines you have read in total and make a note.
※ Count the number of words in three lines and divide by 3 to give you an average.
※ Average number of words x number of lines = words per minute (wpm).
※ Compare this wpm with your previous wpm.

Case study: Creative reading

While working with a client on speed reading, he asked if there was any other way to increase comprehension with information that was more technical and complex (he was studying Nano-technology). During the session I offered him a strategy I called creative reading. The process is pretty straight – forward, however it requires some time and energy. After speed reading a book, there will be areas that you have read which are more complex or technical. Take another pass at the book and this time for each of those areas let your mind actively create visual stories and dial them up 'as they happen'.

This is slightly different to extracting facts and turning them into reference stories. With creative reading you let the stories come to mind in real time, ideally using a range of reading speeds. You could think of it like driving your car on a country road at 50mph and when you come to a town or village slowing down to 30mph or 20mph to take in things of interest.

When you finish reading you probe your mind to recall as many of those images/stories as you can.

For my client he discovered that by practising this strategy he was immediately able to comprehend and remember more of the technical information within the books he was reading. It is now a process, which is second nature for him.

In practice

Like all other strategies in this book, effective speed reading doesn't happen overnight. The good news is, these reading strategies are easy to practise, as you are most likely reading something every day.

TEN-DAY CHALLENGE

Take up the ten-day challenge! Each time you read over the next ten days put some or all of these techniques into practice and check your wpm at the end to measure your improvement.

Focus points

* Find your benchmark so you can track your improvement and increase your motivation.
* Turn on your mental radar by defining your purpose and set yourself up to track down the relevant information.
* Use rapid previewing to build up the 10,000-foot view and identify some of the key nuggets of information.
* At least double your current speed by employing speed reading in your day-to-day life.
* Get out your chopsticks and overcome back-skipping and regression with guiding techniques.
* Engage your peripheral vision by seeing from your mind's eye; use the tangerine technique to get started.
* Practise silent reading and only subvocalizing relevant words, increasing your speed and comprehension.
* Spend time imagining reading at high speed to create solid references in your mind and powerful beliefs that increase your speed.

Next steps

If you give these reading strategies a chance they can literally change your life. As well as the obvious benefits of saving you time and helping to deal with information overload, they offer you a sense of certainty about your ability to learn anything.

In the next week find three books that you have been putting off reading and use these strategies for each one of them. Focus on speed over comprehension to begin with; your purpose here is to get your brain used to a new set of patterns for finding the most relevant information quickly while (with practice) increasing comprehension. To add an extra layer of comprehension for more technical information, practices the art of creative reading.

Part Three
How to remember

'Repetition is the mother of skill.'

Anthony Robbins

10

Lifestyle: Master your memory

In this chapter you will learn:

- ► *how to experience the value of immersion*
- ► *how to get organized with your 'things to do'*
- ► *how to create your mindset for remembering names*
- ► *how to tap into your natural memory for directions.*

Immersion

When put into practice, creative memorization can be a powerful skill in the context of your everyday life. To become skilful at anything you have to use repetition; through repetition you will strengthen your neuronal pathways for that specific skill. Through immersion, actually living with these skills, you work towards mastery and the possibility of creating real change.

The concepts of creative memorization, mind mapping and speed reading can be grasped relatively quickly, but making them part of 'how you think' and putting them into practice so that you gain real value without it being a 'chore', in the beginning at least, can be a challenge.

Key idea: Dealing with setbacks

Like any new skill, you may hit a bump in the road, there might be a temptation to fall back into old habits that are less effective and take what initially feels like the easy route. By immersing yourself in the following techniques, you can cruise over those bumps.

Case study: Immersion

During the game show I created, *Memory Masters*, I ran a two-day seminar with 30 contestants. They then had two weeks to remember a large amount of information. Rather than just running the seminar, then leaving them to create memory networks and reference stories of their own, I would help by breaking down the information into reference stories to give them a 'kick-start', as it were. This meant that by the end of those two weeks their brains were truly immersed in creating these types of pattern, and by the second week, most contestants were substituting my images with their own, which was the goal.

Things to do

It is a short and simple place to start. You already have the skills to remember the things that you need to do. The value comes from asking yourself, 'How can memorizing specific things to do save me time and make me more organized?' Perhaps there are details about upcoming meetings that are useful to be able to call on, maybe there are times when you need to remember things to do from ad hoc conversations, it could be that it is simply a quick way of keeping your skills up to scratch.

Remember this

You don't memorize 'everything' you need to do; focus on tasks that have a higher priority, that are important enough to spend a few minutes putting them onto a memory network. Start the day by memorizing key meetings and tasks; if you're on the move a lot, it creates a sense of control to always know what is coming up next and how one conversation may relate to another conversation happening later that day.

Try it now: What are your reasons?

Time limit: 3 minutes

* What are your reasons for creating 'things to do' memory networks?
* How would you use them in your life?

Once you have compelling reasons for creating your 'things to do' networks, work out how many memory networks you need by classifying them by purpose.

Examples

* *Family*
* *Business*
* *Daily*
* *Events*
* *Ad hoc*

You may choose to create a mind map or other system that captures all of your 'things to do' as well as keeping them on your memory networks.

Try it now: 'Things to do' networks

Time limit: 5 minutes

Choose three categories that make sense for you and create three
separate memory networks with ten nodes in each.

'Things to do' is an easy way to build up your mental muscles
and get yourself in shape for some of the more heavyweight
memorizing.

Names

Key idea: Creating rapport

Whether in social situations or in business, the ability to remember
people's names is something that not only makes a person stand out
and be remembered, but also offers opportunities to create rapport and
build relationships. Everyone likes it when you remember their name; it is
one of the simplest things you can do to demonstrate that you have an
interest in that person.

Unfortunately, not remembering a name is something that can create
many awkward situations. You will no doubt have met people who
announce that they are so bad at remembering names they won't
even try.

Creative memorization presents a process for remembering a
person's name that will vastly increase your chances of 'getting
it right'. It is unlikely that you will remember everyone you
meet; there will be times when the connections you have made
were not strong enough or they have simply faded away. One
day you may remember 30 people in a room, but if you meet
them one month later the connections you made have faded.
The strength of the connection will depend on many factors,
one of the most relevant being 'How important is it that you
remember this person?'

Case study: What's in a name?

I usually start my seminars by memorizing everyone's name, but I don't initially draw attention to it. I meet everyone individually and introduce myself, then after the first 20–30 minutes or so, I start directing thoughts or questions to people in the session using their name. After a short time there is always a small buzz going around the room – 'He knows all our names!' I have tried many variations on memorizing names and so far I have found the strategies I am about to teach you work best. From talking to memory athletes around the world, I know that everyone will have their own 'take' on it. Once you have a solid framework, I would suggest playing with this to find a way that works for you.

MINDSET

You will no doubt have noticed that a pattern is emerging around priming yourself to remember. Memorizing names is slightly different from other kinds of memorizing as you do not tend to have time to prepare, in the same way you could prepare for, let's say, an exam. However, there are ways that you can set yourself up for names; it all comes down to creating the right mindset.

Meeting new people is often unexpected, so remembering their name is sometimes the last thing on your mind. Sometimes the reason you are meeting seems more important than the people you are meeting. In either case it's not so much remembering who they are, as not getting their name to begin with. Sometimes you meet a large group of people all at once and believe there is no way you will remember everyone's name so there doesn't seem any point in trying, and even if you do try, you get the first three or four and then forget them within seconds.

To deal with these challenges you need to construct a specific mindset to remember names and condition it until it becomes instinctive. The correct mindset involves running through a set of steps every time you meet someone; with repetition, the right neuronal networks will fire up instinctively. Make remembering people's names your prime goal; put it right at the top of your list.

Try it now: Condition yourself to remember
Time limit: 5 minutes

Spend time over the next seven days going through this quick action or your own variation of it. Try it now.

✻ As you sit down, become aware of your body in the chair; as your muscles relax, let go of all tension. Focus on your feet and bring your attention up through your calf muscles, past your knees and into your thighs; notice how your legs are relaxing. Enjoy this feeling as it travels up through your hips, waist and into your chest. Become aware of the muscles in your chest and let that awareness drift into your shoulders and down your arms all the way to your fingertips. Let that awareness come back up to your neck and all around your face and head; notice how relaxed you are as you sit in the chair.

✻ Now spend a few minutes thinking about the people you might meet today. Are there people you meet regularly you still don't know yet? What could you do to remember their names? As you think about meeting these people, imagine getting yourself ready to remember them, feel confident that you will find it easy to remember their names and use them naturally in conversation. See yourself in conversation with people throughout the day, remembering their names and notice how they remember yours. Notice that before you meet people, you are already priming yourself to remember their name; you are interested to see how quickly you can memorize it and how long you can retain it. Realize how easy this is and how good it makes you feel.

✻ Spend a few minutes rehearsing meeting people throughout the day and remembering their names effortlessly.

✻ When you have finished, take some deep breaths and feel a relaxing energy coming into your body, setting you up for the day.

Remember this

If all you did was conditioning yourself to remember names, you would notice a big improvement. You can also download a full-length version of this conditioning session from http://improve-your-memory. memoryschool.com.

ATTENTION

Be aware of **where** you met someone as well as **why** you met them. If you can remember the location at a later time, this can help you to remember details about the episode, including their name.

While you are working through the process of conditioning, as soon as you meet a person (even someone you know well), pay attention to how they look. This may feel strange at first and you have to find the balance between paying attention and staring.

Pay attention to the overall look, the shape of their head, shape and colour of eyes, what their ears remind you of, how they move their mouth, whether they have a Roman nose or a large forehead or perhaps they lead with their chin. Study their features and bring that together with their hair, skin colour and type; is it smooth, rough, freckly, etc.? Looking at them as a whole, do they remind you of any kind of animal or famous person that would help you remember them?

Remember this

Next time you sit on the train, start noticing how people look. As an actor I was always pretty used to 'people watching'. As someone who is practising remembering names, it is about finding the differences in how people look and playing with those differences in your mind.

FEATURES

While you are studying a person's face, become aware of their most prominent features and mentally exaggerate them. Create a clear mental image of that person in your mind. Their face will effectively become the 'node' or 'location' that you connect their name to.

Try it now: Exaggerate me!
Time limit: 5 minutes

Get a picture of someone you know well (perhaps go to Facebook or Flickr if you use any of those sites for uploading photographs) and spend five minutes studying people's features and exaggerating them.

LISTEN

There can be embarrassment associated with not hearing a person's name to begin with; sometimes that is through lack of attention and other times it is simply because the person you are speaking to has a name you have never heard before. If you have the right mindset, you should be primed to listen; if you are listening, then you should catch their name in the first place. In the situation where you can't hear the person's name clearly or it is difficult to pronounce, simply ask them to repeat their name or spell it; if you say this out of interest in them, people generally don't mind.

When you hear their name, repeat it back to them out loud: this will make stronger connections with the name and the person. There will be some situations where this may seem awkward; being introduced to a group of people could be one of them. In this case, there are two things you can do:

► Take a chance and memorize their names as quickly as you can: by doing this you should pick up the majority of them. Use people's names early in conversation; if there is one you can't remember, simply ask them again.

► Listen to names being said once and then say to the group as a whole, 'I just want to make sure I have everybody's name', and start running through each one out loud. People will realize if you haven't got it first time round and will tell you their name again. The first method is probably preferable, but if you pull this one off it can be very impressive and you will no doubt be remembered too.

CONNECTION

Almost in parallel with listening to the name, you need to be creating an image for their name, either a sound-image or a natural-image, and making a connection with the feature you have identified. This is probably the most challenging aspect of remembering names, but it is also the part that will enable you to remember 20–50 people in the room.

You will find that with practice, as with numbers, you will start to build up a vocabulary of images to represent names, so if a name is familiar to you, it will be a simple task to create a connection. The challenge happens when you are faced with a name you have never heard before or rarely hear. In these cases you can usually create an image for the first syllable of the name and through using the name in conversation create a strong association with the person. Afterwards you can reinforce the image for when you meet someone with the same name in the future.

Example

If you meet a person called John, there are several images that spring to mind – a john (toilet) or maybe you know someone called John who likes to paint. You could use a paintbrush or a toilet. If John has a prominent forehead, you might imagine him painting it with your favourite colour.

It is always best never to let people know the images you are creating in your mind. Once you get to know the person you won't need to refer to the images, as you will just 'know' their name.

If John's second name was Cartwright, you might imagine him painting his forehead with your favourite colour while lying in a cart – this would all be happening right in front of you.

 Try it now: Remember my name
Time limit: 10 minutes

Using the strategies for names, memorize as many names as you can in 10 minutes.

Alison Shepherd

John Norris

Joseph Pitcher

Carol Williams

Nick Brownlow

Cola Richmond

Caroline Marsden

Emmalene Evans

John Parsonage

Figure 10.1a Memorizing names.

Try it now: Name recall

Time limit: 5 minutes

Write down as many people as you can remember.

Figure 10.1b Recalling names.

If you find you can't immediately recall a name you memorized, ask yourself the question 'What is their name?' and mentally repeat 'Their name will come to me shortly'. As you say this, expect to get an answer. We have all had the experience of seeing someone in the street and you know you know them but the name doesn't come, only for two days later the name to jump back into your head, 'It's John!'

Don't be afraid to fail; play with these techniques and spend some time getting them wrong. As you start to hone your own style, you will notice that the number of names you remember increases.

To remember someone for a longer period of time, find out more details about them; the more you know, the more connections you will make and the easier their name will be to remember.

BUILDING YOUR NETWORK

There can be major benefits and value in knowing people in your network and key facts about them. With social networks such as Twitter, Facebook and LinkedIn, the ability to build that network is easier than it has ever been. The old saying 'It's not what you know but who you know', rings true in a lot of cases; if you have the knowledge and you know the right people, you set yourself up to have a good chance of succeeding in the things you aim to achieve.

As well as building up your personal network, if you are in a career that requires managing a group of stakeholders, it is not only essential that you remember their names, it is beneficial to remember details about what drives them and what their priorities and needs are. Having that information on tap will let you react quickly to situations.

Try it now: Mapping your network
Time limit: 10 minutes

Think about who is in your personal or stakeholder network (you may want to do both).

✳ Create a mind map that puts them into different social groups that could potentially influence your career (employers, employees, partners, opportunities, etc.). If you use something such as Google+, the 'Circles' feature can be very powerful, allowing you to create subsets of your larger circles.

✳ If you manage a group of stakeholders and you are mapping them out, you may want to group them into relevant business areas (product, design, finance, marketing, sales, or whatever structure works for your business).

✳ For each person in your network, what do you know about them? Is there anything that you could offer them that would benefit them? Is there any way that working with someone could be mutually beneficial? Who might be able to utilize your talents?

If you are familiar with the power (the amount of resources a person can bring to a situation) vs interest (their level of commitment) graph, you can use creative memorization to construct a memory network for each quadrant and mentally group the people you need to manage.

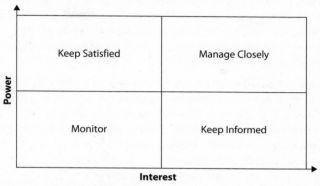

Figure 10.2 Power vs interest graph.

If you have 20 stakeholders, you may have five in each quadrant, for example. If a stakeholder has high power and high interest, they will go in the quadrant that says 'manage closely'. If a person moves, you simply mentally shift them to a different location.

Over time you can build up a set of memory networks that help you store specific information about all of your clients, creating reference stories for their specific challenges and objectives. This is something that can add value to the notes you keep.

Directions

With the huge number of satellite navigation systems available and mapping devices on smart phones, the need to remember directions seems less and less important. There is still an interest in being able to master this skill, though, and potentially it could be essential to your career, if you are planning to become a cab driver, for example, and have to memorize 'The Knowledge'.

Case study: The Knowledge

One of the games in *Memory Masters* was to memorize a large section of 'The Knowledge'; these are the routes London cab drivers have to learn in order to qualify as a driver. Tests have shown that cab drivers have an enlarged hippocampus, the part of the brain that is known to help form episodic memories and is used for spatial memory. You can see what happened here: http://improve-your-memory-memoryschool.com

To remember directions there are two useful steps: prime yourself with the information beforehand and then actually take the journey. With the current technology available in the form of Google Maps streetview, it can be a relatively simple process to memorize the journey beforehand.

Try it now: Holborn to Regent's Park
Time limit: 15 minutes

The following directions are from the AA Routeplanner.

To begin with we will create some codes to represent common words:
* Right – rat
* Left – leaves
* Forward – headbutt

These are examples you can refer to, but where possible try to create your own.

From Holborn–Strand–Covent Garden, London **to** Regent's Park, London

Distance: 2.6 miles Time: 0 hr 12 min

Directions	Reference story	Active testing (out loud)
Start out on Drury Lane, Central London		
Turn right onto Kemble Street	**Kimble** Shanks eating a **Rat**	Drury Lane, turn right onto Kemble Street
Turn left onto the A4200	**RaiN**ing(42) **SauCe**(00) and **Leaves**	Left, A4200
At Holborn Underground Station continue forward onto Southampton Row – A4200	**Headbutt South Ham**	Forward onto Southampton Row
At traffic signals turn left onto the A501		

Signposted Ring Road

	Leaves making a RING	Left, Ring Road

At Euston Underpass continue forward onto the A501

Signposted Ring Road, Marylebone

	Headbutt Mary	Forward, Marylebone
At Great Portland Street Underground Station turn left onto Osnaburgh Street – A4201	Leaves falling on Ice Berg	Left, Osnaburgh Street
At next traffic signals turn right onto the A4201	RatRiNSeD dry	Right, A4201
Take right hand lane and continue forward onto Albany Street - A4201	Headbutt Ale Bee	Forward, Albany
Turn left onto Chester Gate	Leaves on Gate	Left, Chester Gate
Turn right onto Outer Circle	Rats outside a Circle	Right, Outer Circle
Turn left onto Chester Road	Leaves on Chest	Left, Chester
Turn right onto Inner Circle	Rat inside a Circle	Right, Inner Circle

Arrive on Inner Circle

Now that you have primed yourself with the information, you need to associate the reference stories with a memory network. To do this you can use the 'actual locations' found on Google Maps streetview.

The locations will become your memory nodes – Drury Lane, Holborn Station, Euston Underpass, etc.

Example

You go to Google Maps streetview, find the intersection of Drury Lane and Kimble Street, pick a specific point (perhaps the restaurant on the corner) and imagine Kimble Shanks eating a Rat. Continue by associating each one of your reference stories with appropriate locations along the route.

If you don't have access to the internet, you can create your own memory network with 12 nodes (one for each reference story). When you take the journey, simply refer to the stories on your memory network.

If you happen to be learning 'The Knowledge', this is a great way of priming yourself before driving a route and consolidating the information afterwards. It also makes it easy to memorize points of interest along the route, as your route is effectively a memory network.

Physicality

Key idea: Learning physical skills

Creative memorization can play a part in learning a new physical skill, be it a sport, dance routine or even cooking. When learning a physical skill, creative memorization can set up 'markers' or 'visual cues' on your physical journey. These visual cues let you know where you should be at a particular time.

You may be learning to play golf, so you use the chain method to create a set of visual cues that remind you of the grip, stance, backswing, downswing and follow-through. Then by recreating the swing in your mind, you begin to construct a memory of a good golf swing.

Case study: Make 'em laugh

Having been an actor and dancer in a number of London West End shows and on tour, I have had first-hand experience in the application of creative memorization in dance. When I was playing Cosmo in *Singin' in the Rain*, the choreographer Stephen Mear had a vision of what one of the numbers, 'Make 'em Laugh', should be. Rather than working in a strict manner where you memorized the steps, then moved on, he was collaborative to the point where he allowed me to throw out some ideas. In effect he was encouraging the learning cycle. He was able to guide this process until he achieved the results he was looking for. To add to this, in rehearsals I was able to 'imagine' visual cues that triggered the next sequence; this was only needed until I became completely familiar with the routine and it felt like second nature.

As well as creating visual cues, thinking about the learning cycle while learning a new physical activity will help in how quickly you pick it up. Find what is similar in this new skill to others you have practised in the past. Play with your own ideas and experiment through trial, error and repetition, honing and adapting as you go.

For anything that requires remembering physical movements, you are generally dealing with procedural memories, relying on what you unconsciously know and building on this. If, for example, you are a martial artist in wing chun and someone shows you a unique combination of moves that are made up of techniques you have previously learned, you will find it easier to remember than someone who has never done wing chun but has practised karate for a number of years.

Rehearsal is key in any physical activity you are involved in, not just going through the movements but getting every fibre of your being involved; by this very essence you are creating a multitude of memorable connections.

Focus points

* Repetition is the mother of skill: immerse yourself in creative memorization to take you on the road to mastery.
* Gently build up your memory muscles, classifying your 'things to do' and creating a structure to get things done.
* Make remembering names part of your day-to-day mindset; condition yourself to remember names for the next seven days.
* Pay attention to the details: remember where and why as well as the person's overall look.
* Use creative memorization and make names through exaggeration, listening and connection.
* Build a network of people that will be mutually beneficial and practise your skills by remembering key information.
* If you manage stakeholders, capture them on a mind map and memorize them depending on their level of power vs interest.
* Use creative memorization to memorize directions quickly with the aid of Google Maps.
* Take advantage of visual cues in learning physical skills such as dance, sport and cooking.

Next steps

Find the simple daily activities you can do that give you small consistent results. Building on these will allow you to immerse yourself into a new way of thinking about how you use your memory in your everyday life.

Take some time to pull out some specific examples of activities you will try within the next seven days.

11

General knowledge: Sowing the seeds of knowledge

In this chapter you will learn:

- ► *how to prime yourself for knowledge*
- ► *how to remember facts and figures*
- ► *how to make complex information easy to remember*
- ► *how to remember and cook your favourite recipes.*

Key idea: Learning factual information

The ability to reel off general knowledge in itself can be very impressive. By exploring how to memorize different types of factual information, you allow your brain to immerse itself in the practice of creative memorization, working towards a point where it becomes second nature.

With this chapter you should initially read through it to get a sense of what it entails, then work through the 'activities' that you feel you will get the most value from, using it as a resource you can come back to again and again.

One of the best known memory champions of all time, Dominic O'Brien, is renowned for many record-breaking memory feats. In his earlier days he even memorized all of the questions and answers to Trivial Pursuits, accumulating a mass of general knowledge.

Sowing the seeds

Remember this

By taking time to remember general knowledge, you are effectively sowing the seeds that will set you up for similar knowledge in the future. If, for example, you know that Ryan Lochte set a world record at the 2011 World Swimming Championships for the 200 metres individual medley with a time of 1:54.00, if you saw him swim in the 2012 Olympics you would have had a point of reference and an opportunity to connect more information when he placed silver with a time of 1:54:09 losing out to Michael Phelps. The simple fact of knowing the time to beat can also change your emotional engagement with any events which Ryan Lochte and his famous arch-rival Michael Phelps participate in. Since you are primed you will 'notice' more stories about their rivalry than you might have otherwise. By having an emotional engagement and being primed in this way, your brain will naturally be directing your attention to remember more and the information becomes relevant and interesting. The ideas that you have sown here grow as you naturally make more connections.

For most of the 'activities' you will go through in this chapter, you will need to create memory networks to store the information. It is recommended that you spend some time brainstorming events in your life from which you can construct memory networks. Alternatively, a quick and easy way (as mentioned previously) is to use Google Maps to construct your memory networks. In some cases there will be a more natural memory network to store the information, as with oceans.

Remember this

While going through the activities in this chapter, reflect on any similarities there are between the information you have to learn in your current role. Think of the best ways you could structure your own information and how you could utilize these same types of strategy.

Geography

Geography is a complex and wide-ranging topic. For the purposes of putting creative memorization into practice we will look at a simple and very small slice that demonstrates how to remember some facts in relation to oceans and mountains of the world.

Try it now: Oceans and mountains

Time limit: 20 minutes

* Rather than creating an unrelated memory network for the oceans, a more natural method is simply to get a globe and in the Pacific create your reference story, using your natural spatial memory to 'see' where the Pacific is.
* With mountains you may want initially to create a memory network as a point of reference until you just 'know' where they are.
* For each example, create the images clearly in your mind and associate to your memory node.

Example

Pacific is the memory node – imagine Mariana eating a Meal that is Funky in the middle of the Pacific. Make it real and dial up the intensity, recite aloud 'Pacific – Deepest point – Mariana Trench 35,827 ft.'

Oceans – deepest point	Reference story (examples)
Pacific – Mariana Trench – 35,827 ft	**Mariana** eating a **MeaL**(35) that is **FuNKy**(827)
Atlantic – Puerto Rico Trench – 30,246 ft	**Sharks** (West Side Story) fighting hol**MeS**(30) with e**NeRGy**(246)
Indian – Java Trench – 24,460 ft	Cup of **Java** drunk by he**NRy**(24) with **RoaCHeS**(460)
Southern – Southern Ocean – 23,737 ft	The Southerner **NeMoy**(23) reading a **CoMiC**(737)
Arctic – Arctic Basin – 18,456 ft	Basin with a **DoVe**(18) in **ReLiSH**(456)

For mountains we will create a code for the various countries:

✽ Nepal/Tibet – NuT

✽ Pakistan/China – PaC

✽ India/Nepal – IaN

You might imagine yourself on the top of **Everest** with only **NuT**s around your neck. While having a **NaP**(29), **SN**oo**Py**(029) licks your face.

Mountains (all Himalayas – except K2)	Reference story (your stories)
Everest – Nepal/Tibet – 29,029 ft	
K2 – Karakoram – Pakistan/China – 28,251 ft	
Kanchenjunga – India/Nepal – 28,169 ft	
Lhotse – Nepal/Tibet – 27,940 ft	
Makalu – Nepal/Tibet – 27,838 ft	
Cho Oyu – Nepal/Tibet – 26,864 ft	
Dhaulagiri – Nepal – 26,795 ft	
Manaslu – Nepal – 26,781 ft	
Nanga Parbat – Pakistan – 26,660 ft	
Annapurna – Nepal – 26,545 ft	

Entertainment

The next activity is specifically designed to test your mental stamina: remembering every single best picture Oscar winner dating back to 1927–8.

Try it now: Oscar winners, Best Picture
Time limit: 30 minutes (examples)

There are several methods of memorizing Best Picture Oscar winners. You could associate the name of the movie with the year on its own without using a memory network or associate the movie with the year and then connect to a memory network node:

Memory node: Chair, Movie – Date: 1927–8, *Wings*

A **NaVy** Seal with **Wings** sitting on your **Chair**

Or since the data is in chronological order you could construct a memory network in such a way that it is easy to find a particular number by chunking up your nodes (refer to *How to memorize a memory network* in the 'Try it now' box in Chapter 6).

Chunk of 6: → 28, 29, 30, 31, 32, 33 (*these are the non-calendar years 27/28, etc.*)

Chunk of 7: → 34, 35, 36, 37, 38, 39, 40 (*by taking your second chunk up to 40 the years following this will be easier to remember*)

Chunk of 5: → 41, 42, 43, 44, 45 (*continue with chunks of 5*)

*You know that your first node (**Chair**) is number 27/28 – the chair has **Wings**.*

Using this approach, you would only need to associate the name of the movie to your node, rather than the movie and the year. You will have to spend more time learning where the numbers are.

I have given examples using the first approach back to 1971 (the year I was born).

Oscar winners	Reference story (examples)
2010 – *The King's Speech*	The King with a DaZzling(10) Crown
2009 – *The Hurt Locker*	Rubbing SoaP(09) on The Hurt Locker
2008 – *Slumdog Millionaire*	Actor from Slumdog breaking into a SaFe(08)
2007 – *No Country for Old Men*	Old Men carrying SaCKs(07)
2006 – *The Departed*	The Departed lying in SewaGe(06)
2005 – *Crash*	A Crashed SaiL(05)
2004 – *Million Dollar Baby*	Million Dollar Baby is SoRe(04)
2003 – *The Lord of the Rings: The Return of the King*	Gollum fighting SaM(03) in Return of the King
2002 – *Chicago*	Chicago and SiN(02)
2001 – *A Beautiful Mind*	A Beautiful Mind that is SaD(01)
2000 – *Gladiator*	Gladiator covered in SauCe(00)
1999 – *American Beauty*	American Beauty is a BaBe(99)
1998 – *Shakespeare in Love*	Shakespeare at a BuFfet(98)

(Continued)

Oscar winners	Reference story (examples)
1997 – *Titanic*	Titanic is BiG(97) or ePiC(97)
1996 – *The English Patient*	The English Patient is PoSH(96)
1995 – *Braveheart*	Braveheart does BaLLet(95)
1994 – *Forrest Gump*	Forrest Gump loves a PeaR(94)
1993 – *Schindler's List*	Schindler's List goes BooM(93)
1992 – *Unforgiven*	Unforgiven ends up in the BiN(92)
1991 – *The Silence of the Lambs*	Hannibal is scary with his BaT(91)
1990 – *Dances with Wolves*	Dancing Wolves playing the BaSS(90)
1989 – *Driving Miss Daisy*	Driving Miss Daisy is PHoeBe(89)
1988 – *Rain Man*	Rain Man in ViVa(88) Las Vegas
1987 – *The Last Emperor*	The Last Emperor in the FoG(87)
1986 – *Platoon*	Platoon on a VoyaGe(86)
1985 – *Out of Africa*	FaLL(85) Out of Africa
1984 – *Amadeus*	Amadeus playing on a FeRRy(84)
1983 – *Terms of Endearment*	Shirley MacLaine of huge FaMe(83)
1982 – *Gandhi*	Gandhi surrounded by FaNs(82)
1981 – *Chariots of Fire*	Chariots of Fire racing bareFooT(81)
1980 – *Ordinary People*	Ordinary Person with an extraordinary FaCe(80)
1979 – *Kramer vs. Kramer*	Kramers fighting in a CaB(79)
1978 – *The Deer Hunter*	The Deer Hunter gun scene set in a café(78)
1977 – *Annie Hall*	Annie Hall baking a CaKe(77)
1976 – *Rocky*	Rocky in a CaGe(76)
1975 – *One Flew over the Cuckoo's Nest*	Nicholson with a CLaw(75)
1974 – *The Godfather, Part II*	The Godfather in a ChoiR(74)
1973 – *The Sting*	The Sting covered in GuM(73)
1972 – *The Godfather*	The Godfather in aGoNy(72)
1971 – *The French Connection*	The French CaDDy(71)
1970 – *Patton*	
1969 – *Midnight Cowboy*	
1968 – *Oliver!*	
1967 – *In the Heat of the Night*	
1966 – *A Man for All Seasons*	
1965 – *The Sound of Music*	
1964 – *My Fair Lady*	
1963 – *Tom Jones*	
1962 – *Lawrence of Arabia*	
1961 – *West Side Story*	
1960 – *The Apartment*	
1959 – *Ben-Hur*	

1958 – *Gigi*
1957 – *The Bridge on the River Kwai*
1956 – *Around the World in 80 Days*
1955 – *Marty*
1954 – *On the Waterfront*
1953 – *From Here to Eternity*
1952 – *The Greatest Show on Earth*
1951 – *An American in Paris*
1950 – *All About Eve*
1949 – *All the King's Men*
1948 – *Hamlet*
1947 – *Gentleman's Agreement*
1946 – *The Best Years of Our Lives*
1945 – *The Lost Weekend*
1944 – *Going My Way*
1943 – *Casablanca*
1942 – *Mrs. Miniver*
1941 – *How Green Was My Valley*
1940 – *Rebecca*
1939 – *Gone with the Wind*
1938 – *You Can't Take It with You*
1937 – *The Life of Emile Zola*
1936 – *The Great Ziegfeld*
1935 – *Mutiny on the Bounty*
1934 – *It Happened One Night*
1932/33 – *Cavalcade*
1931/32 – *Grand Hotel*
1930/31 – *Cimarron*
1929/30 – *All Quiet on the Western Front*
1928/29 – *The Broadway Melody*
1927/28 – *Wings*

History

History is all about stories and is therefore a great fit for creative memorization. To help with the process there is usually a wealth of imagery online that can be used in your reference stories. The statue of Pytheas for example could be used as the image for Pytheas; if you need an image to help remember his name, you might simply imagine him eating a pie – with repetition you will just know the statue is Pytheas.

Try it now: Historical facts

Time limit: 30 minutes

With historical facts it can be useful to create your reference stories to begin with and then choose one key image to store on a memory network. This will allow you to run through in sequence. When you see Pytheas on the memory node, your memory recalls the reference story of Pytheas sailing around the British Isles.

This also has the benefit of being able to memorize information as and when you need it and arrange it in a structured sequence at a later date.

Example

Memory node 1: Pytheas → remember reference story

Memory node 2: Camulodunum

Memory node 3: Hadrian

British timeline	Reference story (examples)
330–320BC – Pytheas of Massilia (now Marseilles) – Greek merchant and explorer circumnavigated the British Isles – produced the first written record of the islands.	**Pytheas** (statue) sailing around the **British Isles** with a gigantic **written record** of the islands. On the ship is MuMS(330) MiNCe(320).
AD43 – British capital Camulodunum (Colchester) falls to the Romans and Emperor Claudius.	Camulodunum is being held in the enormous clawed hand of Claudius from RoMe(43).
AD122 – Emperor Hadrian orders the construction of a wall across northern Britain.	Hadrian's Wall is covered in TaNNiN(122).
843 – Kenneth MacAlpine unites Scots and Picts in a 'kingdom of Scotland'.	Kenneth MacAlpine on a FaRM(843) hugging a Scot and a Pict forming a Kingdom.
1042 – Edward the Confessor becomes King of England.	
1190 – Richard I joins the Third Crusade.	
23 August 1305 – Scottish rebel William Wallace is executed by the English.	
1315–1322 – Millions die in the Great European Famine.	
1337 – Hundred Years War between England and France begins.	

1509 – Henry VII dies and is succeeded by Henry VIII.

1580 – Francis Drake arrives at Plymouth after circumnavigating the world.

1651 – Oliver Cromwell defeats Charles II at the Battle of Worcester.

1694 – Bank of England is established.

1768 – Captain James Cook leads his first expedition to the Pacific.

1807 – Britain abolishes the slave trade.

1903 – Women's Social and Political Union is formed to campaign for women's suffrage.

Source: http://www.bbc.co.uk/history

Literature

As a way to begin priming yourself for the works of Shakespeare, first start by memorizing the titles and most likely dates of his plays (it is not really known with any certainty when each play was written but the list below is based on widely held opinion). You could choose to create a memory network on which to store them. You then have the option to associate the relevant characters and plot to each play.

Try it now: Shakespeare

Time limit: 1 hour

* Create a memory network that you can chunk into three (comedies, tragedies and histories).
* All comedies in this list except the last four are dated 15__; you therefore need to associate only the last two digits to the name of the play (you can use this same idea with the other sections).

Comedies	Reference story (examples)
1591 – *The Comedy of Errors*	BaT(91) a **Comedy** with lots of **Errors**
1591 – *The Two Gentlemen of Verona*	BaTs(91) being handed to **Two** handy looking **Gentlemen**
1594 – *The Merchant of Venice*	Lots of **BeeR**(94) being drunk by the **Merchant** in **Venice**
1594 – *A Midsummer Night's Dream*	An **Ass** drinking BeeR(94)

1594 – *The Taming of the Shrew*	**Taming** the **Shrew** with BeeR(94)
1598 – *All's Well That Ends Well*	A slice of **BeeF**(98) that has **ended well**
1598 – *As You Like It*	**You like** this BeeF(98)
1598 – *Love's Labour's Lost*	**BeeF**(98) looking for its **lost love**
1599 – *The Merry Wives of Windsor*	The **Merry Wives of Windsor**, with lots of **BaBies**(99)
1599 – *Twelfth Night,* or *What You Will*	A **BaBe**(99) all alone on **Twelfth Night**
1600 – *Much Ado About Nothing*	**Much Ado** about SauCe(00) being spilt
1604 – *Measure for Measure*	**Measuring** SiR(04)
1610 – *The Winter's Tale*	In **Winter** a **Tale** made of DaiSies(10)
1611 – *The Tempest*	**Temp**ted by TeD(11)

<table>
<tr><td>Tragedies</td><td>Reference story (your stories)</td></tr>
</table>

1591 – *The Tragedy of Romeo and Juliet*	
1592 – *The Tragedy of Titus Andronicus*	
1599 – *The Tragedy of Hamlet, Prince of Denmark*	
1599 – *The Tragedy of Julius Caesar*	
1602 – *The History of Troilus and Cressida*	
1604 – *The Tragedy of Othello, The Moor of Venice*	
1605 – *The Tragedy of King Lear*	
1606 – *The Tragedy of Macbeth*	
1607 – *The Life of Timon of Athens*	
1607 – *The Tragedy of Antony and Cleopatra*	
1608 – *Pericles, Prince of Tyre*	
1608 – *The Tragedy of Coriolanus*	
1610 – *The Tragedy of Cymbeline*	
1613 – *The Two Noble Kinsmen*	

<table>
<tr><td>Histories</td><td>Reference story (your stories)</td></tr>
</table>

1592 – *The First Part of King Henry the Sixth*

1593 – *The Tragedy of Richard the Third, With the Landing of Earl Richmond and the Battle at Bosworth Field*

1593 – *The Second Part of King Henry the Sixth*

1595 – *The Third Part of King Henry the Sixth*

1596 – *The Life and Death of King John*

1597 – *The Tragedy of King Richard the Second*

1597 – *The First Part of King Henry the Fourth*

1597 – *The Second Part of King Henry the Fourth*

1599 – *The Life of Henry the Fifth*

1613 – *The Life of King Henry the Eighth*

Science and nature

THE BRAIN

The brain is a complex structure of neuronal networks, entwining, overlapping and connecting to form specific brain structures. Although not essential in order for you to improve your memory, being able to remember what some of those structures are, and their purpose, will prime you to build future knowledge about the brain.

Try it now: Journey through the brain
Time limit: 15 minutes

These represent a few structures of the brain and some of their functions. Create a memory network consisting of three locations and the appropriate number of items in each location.

Brain structures	Reference story (examples)
Location 1: The brain stem (connects the brain and spinal cord)	Stem connecting the brain and spinal cord
Item 1: Medulla – respiration, heart, gastrointestinal functions	Medal, breathing with a beating heart
Item 2: Pons – interconnects brain stem and cerebellum	Pins, connecting the stem and small brain
Item 3: Midbrain – control of movement	Midfielder controlling movement

Brain structures	Reference story (your stories)
Location 2: Cerebellum – sensory motor co-ordination, seems to play an important role in learning	

Brain structures	Reference story (your stories)
Location 3: Cerebrum – (forebrain) overlies the lower structures	
Item 1: Thalamus – relay station for sensory experience that projects to cerebral cortex	
Item 2: Hypothalamus – master control centre for emotion	
Item 3: Amygdala (limbic) – emotional learning, fear, importance; involved Pavlovian conditioning, influences how memory is stored	
Item 4: Hippocampus (limbic) – key role in forming declarative memories	

(Continued)

Item 5: **Fornix (limbic)** – interconnecting structures of the limbic system

Item 6: **Basal ganglia** – integration of motor activity

Item 7: **Cerebral cortex** – covers the cerebrum; high-level brain functions – thoughts, reasoning, planning, decision-making and imagination

PERIODIC TABLE

Earlier in this book you had a taster of how to remember the elements of the periodic table using the chain method. It can also be helpful to use a memory network onto which you can associate more information in the future.

Try it now: The elements

Time limit: 30 minutes

* Create a memory network for as many elements as you wish to remember (at least 30).

* Use the number of the node of the memory network to represent the atomic number. This means you will not have to create a separate image for the number, e.g. Boron will be on your fifth node, therefore its atomic number is 5.

* Create one image per element.

Elements of the periodic table

Atomic no. – Symbol – Element	Reference story (examples)
1 – H – Hydrogen	Hydrogen bomb
2 – He – Helium	Helium balloon
3 – Li – Lithium	Lithium floating in water
4 – Be – Beryllium	Bee
5 – B – Boron	Boar
6 – C – Carbon	Car
7 – N – Nitrogen	Nitro
8 – O – Oxygen	Oxygen mask
9 – F – Fluorine	Flower reacting violently
10 – Ne – Neon	Neon sign
11 – Na – Sodium	Soda

12 – Mg – Magnesium	Magazine
13 – Al – Aluminium	Aluminium
14 – Si – Silicon	Silly cone
15 – P – Phosphorus	Fozzy
16 – S – Sulphur	Smelly Sulphur
17 – Cl – Chlorine	Chlorine gas
18 – Ar – Argon	Aga oven
19 – K – Potassium	Pot
20 – Ca – Calcium	Milk
21 – Sc – Scandium	Scan
22 – Ti – Titanium	Titanium clubs
23 – V – Vanadium	Van
24 – Cr – Chromium	Chrome wheels
25 – Mn – Manganese	Man on knees
26 – Fe – Iron	Iron man
27 – Co – Cobalt	Cobbles
28 – Ni – Nickel	A nickel
29 – Cu – Copper	Copper
30 – Zn – Zinc	Piece of zinc

Sports and leisure

Depending on the circles you frequent, the ability to pull out facts about sport can be a useful one. As well as demonstrating your knowledge, it is probably one of the more fun areas to be able to share information about.

Try it now: World records at the Olympics
Time limit: 30 minutes

If you choose to put these on a memory network, create one specifically for world records achieved at the Beijing Olympic Games in 2008 and another for 2012. This will help you separate them in your mind.

World records at the 2008 Olympics	Reference stories (examples)
100 metres (athletics) 9.69 seconds Usain Bolt (Jamaica)	**Usain Bolt** wearing **Jamaican** flag doing the 100 metres like Charlie **CHaPlin**(69)
200 metres individual medley (swimming) 1:54.23 Michael Phelps (USA)	**Michael Phelps** wearing **USA** flag swimming against Swans with Medals (number shape system **2** – 200 metres), who were paid a **DoLLaR**(1:54) from **NeMo**(23) to take a dive
Men's 4 km team pursuit (cycling) 3:53.31 Ed Clancy, Bradley Wiggins, Paul Manning, Geraint Thomas (UK)	*Note: Use the 'real people' and memorize their names separately.* A **4**seater bike, with **Ed**, **Bradley**, **Paul** and **Geraint** hanging off different parts, they eMaiL (3:5) a MohaMaD (3:31)
Men's 85 kg total (weightlifting) 394 kg Andrei Rybakou (Belarus)	**Andrei** lifting huge dumbBells (Belarus) on top of the Eiffel(85) Tower in front of the eMPiRe(394)
World records at the 2012 Olympics (Create a new memory network for the equivalent events from 2012)	**Reference story (your stories)**
100 metres (athletics) 9.63 seconds Usain Bolt (Jamaica)	
200 metres individual medley (swimming) 1:54.27 Michael Phelps (USA)	
Men's 4 km team pursuit (cycling) 3:53.29 Ed Clancy, Steven Burke, Peter Kennaugh, Geraint Thomas (UK)	
Men's 85 kg total (weightlifting) 385 kg Adrian Edward ZIELINSKI (Pol)	

RECIPES

The ability to remember recipes has a real practical value in everyday life. With creative memorization you can use memory networks to initially memorize the ingredients needed for a particular recipe and then use a combination of visual cues and physical rehearsal to remember the actual preparation. By going through this process, you are engaging several different types of memory: semantic, episodic and procedural.

Try it now: Spanish chicken and chorizo (by Phil Poole)

Time limit: 30 minutes

This will break down into two parts:

* Create a memory network and memorize the ingredients.
* Create a set of visual cues using the chain method that you can use to physically and mentally rehearse the preparation in order to consolidate this recipe to memory.

Ingredients	Reference story (examples)
4 chicken breasts	**Chicken Breasts on a Door (4)**
1 chorizo ring	a **Chorizo Ring**
1 can of chopped tomatoes	**Chopped Tomatoes**
3 bay leaves	**Bay Leaves** on a **Tree (3)**
1-2 tablespoon of paprika	Tablespoon of **Paprika**
1/4 teaspoon of chilli	Teaspoon of **Chilli**
For the garnish	Reference story (your stories)
70ml (1/4 cup) of dry sherry or vermouth	
1 red pepper	
1 yellow pepper	
1 red onion	
1-2 cloves garlic	
2 packets of rocket leaves	
1 tablespoon of olive oil Pinch of pepper and salt	
To serve	Reference story (your stories)
For something more substantial serve with crunchy fresh bread or garlic bread if you are feeling really decadent.	

Source: www.welovenicethings.com

Preparation method

For each instruction use the chain method to set your visual cues and rehearse preparing the meal.

* Slice the peppers and onion roughly, crush the garlic clove(s), slice the chicken breasts into two chunks.
* Put the casserole dish on the hob on medium heat and add the olive oil; once heated add the chicken breast and brown on all sides for 2-3 minutes. Remove to a spare plate.

✳ Add the garlic, peppers and onion to the oil and cook in the oil until soft (about 3-5 minutes).

✳ Add the chicken breast back in along with the chopped tomatoes and sherry. Also add the paprika, chilli powder, salt and pepper. Once the mixture is bubbling, reduce heat so it is simmering and place lid on.

✳ After 20 minutes stir the mixture and taste, add more paprika and (sparingly) chilli to taste, simmer for another 20 minutes with lid on.

✳ The tomato sauce will now have reduced to a lovely gloopy mess. Slice the chorizo ring and add to dish and simmer for another 5 minutes with lid on.

✳ Remove from heat, add a bed of rocket leaves on each serving dish, add 2-3 chicken pieces on top and then add a mixture of the tomato sauce, peppers, onion and chorizo on and around the leaves and serve.

On the same memory network after the ingredients connect these three chains:

1 *Imagine slicing the rough peppers and onion who crush garlic over the two chunks of chicken.*

2 *A huge casserole dish with oil has a chicken breast swimming in it that is brown, it jumps onto a plate.*

3 *Garlic, peppers and onion jump into the hot oil and start swimming with MaiL (3-5).*

4 *Chicken jumps out of the MaiL and puts chopped tomotoes into a bottle of sherry, the sherry is itchy and covered in paprika, chilli, salt and pepper. Everything starts bubbling, you throw a lid on it.*

5 *A NaSa (20) ship crashes into the lid and starts sipping the contents*

6 *It takes slices of chorizo and covers with a SaiL (05).*

7 *You pick it up and drop on a bed of rocket leaves, the chicken jumps on top, the sauce dripping around it.*

In practice

Put your knowledge to the test and see how well you score on the 'How to Remember' pub quiz.

Try it now: Pub quiz

Time limit: 10 minutes

Test your knowledge with our pub quiz.

1 Which ocean has the deepest trench?
2 How many bay leaves are in Spanish chicken and chorizo?
3 Out of the first 30 elements on the periodic table, name how many have a symbol starting with the letter C.
4 Name the four athletes who broke the world record for the men's 4km team pursuit at the Beijing Olympics.
5 Is it the hypothalamus or the hippocampus that has a key role in forming declarative memories?
6 Which three plays is Shakespeare thought to have written in 1591?
7 What year were the hills alive with the *Sound of Music* at the Oscars?
8 Where and in what year did Francis Drake arrive after circumnavigating the world?
9 Put these mountains in order of highest to lowest: Nanga Parbat, Kanchenjunga, Annapurna.
10 What element comes after iron in the periodic table and what is its symbol and number?
11 Which of the following parts of the brain controls sensory motor skills: amygdala, cerebellum, medulla?
12 How many packets of rocket leaves are needed for the garnish?
13 Who won the men's 85k total (weightlifting) in 2012?
14 When is Shakespeare thought to have written *Hamlet* and what year did the film win the Oscar?
15 In which year did the English execute William Wallace and in what year did the film about his life win the Oscar?
16 How many histories did Shakespeare write about a Henry?
17 Britain abolished the slave trade in which year: 1807, 1808, or 1809?
18 How many minutes do you simmer the Spanish chicken and chorizo for?
19 Usain Bolt set a world record at the Beijing Olympics, running the 100 metres in how many seconds?
20 *The Godfather* won the Oscar for best film in 1974, 1973, or 1972?

Focus points

* Learn and grow future general knowledge by sowing the seeds today.
* Take creative memorization to the next level by immersing yourself in the memorization of complex facts, numbers and dates.
* There are various methods for remembering general knowledge across a variety of areas: geography, entertainment, history, literature, science and nature, and sports and leisure.
* You can use creative memorization to remember the ingredients and also how to cook your favourite recipes.
* Go memorize a set of trivial pursuit questions and answers!

Next steps

You may already naturally consume general knowledge, however if this is one of your first steps into taking a more structured approach, think about the areas that interest you and set aside some time to hunt down some facts. Start small, search out 10 facts in a week and look at where you can bring them up or put them to some fun use.

12

Programming to remember: Take control of your memory

In this chapter you will learn:

- ▶ *how to remember where you've put things using mental tags*
- ▶ *games to condition your memory*
- ▶ *how to programme future memories.*

There will always be things that we forget, whether it is where we've put something or the 'important' task we we're 'supposed' to do. A lot of the time this is due to lack of attention or our attention being diverted. However, there are things we can do to increase our awareness and remember those things that make us go 'doh!'

The past: Where did I put my keys?

It's a cliché, but the thought behind it stands true. I am sure that at one or perhaps many times in your life you have experienced the 'Where did I put my keys?' scenario. It can be fairly frustrating; you 'know' you left your keys on the kitchen table, you search everywhere for them, someone must have moved them, you search everywhere again, you think about what you were wearing last time you had them, ten minutes go by and now you are late, then your partner finds them on the bookshelf, 'Ah, now I remember.'

Case study: How forgetful is the UK as a nation?

Research conducted by Sight Station Fashion Reading Glasses in 2014 of a nationally representative sample of 1,000 UK adults, aimed to reveal how forgetful the UK is as a nation, what we find hardest to remember, and what items we lose most frequently. Statistics showed that 78 per cent surveyed were more likely to have lost items including keys, socks and reading glasses as opposed to items like wedding rings, wallets and cameras. It also showed that 80 per cent of us spend up to 20 minutes a day searching for lost or misplaced items. On average we are spending 41 minutes a week, 3 hours a month, 35.5 hours a year searching for lost or misplaced items. Over one third of those who responded said they do nothing to improve their memory. The ones who do, played brain games such as Sudoku (41 per cent) or writing lists (36 per cent) and making habits such as putting possessions in the same place every time (24 per cent).

There is a strategy you can play with that will make a shift in how you think about this specific scenario, how you deal with it and the outcome. The strategy is simple and you have more than enough skills to put it into practice.

In effect you are aiming to set yourself up to remember. To do this there has to be a conscious effort when you put something down (your keys in this case); by conditioning yourself to do this, over time it will become an unconscious habit.

The outcome of this is that more and more you will be able to remember where you put things. You may find that when this starts to work for you, you use the same or a similar technique to remember other things that happen, not just where you put things but small moments or events. While moments and events can be memorable within themselves, by mentally 'tagging' them, you can make them stand out in your memory.

Try it out: Creating your tag

Time limit: 2 minutes

The idea of this exercise is that you start to condition yourself to remember things you've done in the past. Start small and just try this every time you put something down that you will need later.

* Create a tag-word – this could be something as simple as 'down'; practise saying it out loud in a specific way.
* Create a physical action to go with this tag-word – you might touch the object with two fingers in a specific way.
* Create an image you can see in your mind – you might imagine an alien substance reaching up from wherever the object is and grabbing it down tightly.
* To put this into practice fire off all three things at the same time.

Example

Try this with your phone or keys: put the item down on the table top, then as you touch it with your two fingers and say the word 'down' imagine the alien substance grabbing it – this should all happen fairly instantaneously. Do this five times.

Another option is to make something up on the spot. You put your keys down beside the microwave – imagine they go smashing through the microwave (the microwave screams); this image will stand out in your mind when you next think of your keys.

When you next think of your phone or keys, you will remember this moment and therefore remember where they are. The problem is that you may forget to do this, which is why you need to condition yourself to do it without thinking. You can do this by taking one to three items that you know you put down at least three or four times a day, and spend the next seven days tagging those items; for this to work you have to make a conscious effort.

Try it now: Find the blank
Time limit: 10 mins, played over the course of 1 week

There is a simple game you can play that will help condition your memory in this area. It's also fun – and if you are the person who gets asked a lot 'Where's my _____?', you will love this game. It is aimed at couples or families; you could play it on your own but you would always win.

Rules
✻ The game lasts a week, starting on Monday and finishing on Sunday.
✻ The names of the players are written on a piece of A4 paper and pinned to a wall.
✻ Whenever anyone says 'Where's my _____?' or words to that effect, they have 5 minutes in which to find it. If they find it, then nothing is marked on the board; but if they don't, an X goes down (maximum of three Xs in one day or there is a consequence – you decide).
✻ If they haven't found it after 5 minutes, everyone else joins in the search; you get an extra life if you find it (a star or a tick) that you can use to get rid of a future X you may pick up.
✻ The person with the most Xs at the end of the week gets a penalty – they might pay for a meal out or a movie, or if you have children you could dream up some fun chores.

If you have a family, this can be quite amusing; the interesting thing is how quickly you get conditioned to remember where you have put stuff. Combine this with the tag-word strategy and you will find that forgetting where things are is a thing of the past.

PLAY THE TIMELINE

If you find that even with tagging you are still not able to remember, next time you forget where something is, rather than looking all over the house, take a moment, breathe deeply, let yourself relax and then ask the question 'Where are my _____?' Ask the question with the expectation that you will get an answer and then let your mind drift and take you back to the point where you last remember having them; remember this time in detail. When you have that picture clear in your mind, start to play the timeline forward as far as you can until you remember where they last were.

With this technique you may find that half-way through, the location of your item suddenly pops into your mind. You are essentially looking for connections, trying to spark off the same neuronal pathways that were created when you put that item down.

The future: Don't forget the milk!

There are many occasions when you want to remember something at a specific time in the future; in order to do this something has to trigger that memory. By creating future memory through creative memorization, you can effectively make suggestions to your unconscious mind, programming yourself to remember the thing you want to do at an event in the future.

You could think of it like getting notifications pushed to your phone; in the same way, your unconscious can metaphorically 'push' actions to your conscious when triggered by an event.

Try it now: Creating your anchor
Time limit: 5 minutes

This technique works in a similar way to the technique for creating a tag. The difference being that rather than create a memory for where something is right now, we will remember it at a future time. With your anchor you are creating a memory for a future event that will be unconsciously triggered when that event happens.

Example
You want to remember to pick up a pint of milk when you finish work.

✻ Create an anchor word – let's use 'Remember'. Practise saying it aloud in a specific way.

✻ Create a physical action to go with it – maybe a 'click' of the fingers.

✻ Create a future memory – imagine as you step off your train and put your ticket through the ticket barrier you see an enormous pint of milk running up to hug you.

✻ Once the image is clear in your mind, fire off all three together – see the story and as soon as the enormous milk comes into it say 'Remember milk' and click your fingers on the word 'milk'.

You may find that, as you get off the train, milk will pop into your head before you get to the ticket barrier. If this happens, it's important that you keep it in your mind until you get there. More often than not the memory will be triggered either before or just at the right moment.

Like the first technique, this one will take some practice: you should aim to use it at least one to five times a day for the first seven days in order to condition it into your way of thinking.

Remember this

Although this technique is really simple, I still find it impressive when just at the right moment the memory pops into my head. One of the side-effects of both of these techniques is that they create some very strong references in your ability to remember. With strong references you create strong beliefs and with a belief in your abilities your memory will continue to improve.

Focus points

✳ Practise using the tag technique: fire off a physical action, key word and visual image simultaneously to remember where you have put things.

✳ Take the seven-day challenge and condition yourself to tag where you put your relevant possessions without thinking.

✳ Play the 'Find the Blank' game as a fun way to improve your skills with the tag technique.

✳ Try using the timeline technique, taking yourself back to a time when you last had the object you have forgotten and imagine running the timeline forward.

✳ Create an anchor for remembering things you have to do in the future by having a key word, physical action and a future memory. Program yourself by firing off all three together.

✳ Practise programming yourself with future memories.

Next steps

While the ultimate value of being able to remember your keys or program yourself to buy some milk may seem limited, by conditioning your mind to think in this way you are creating some very powerful habits that not only create momentum to help you become more observant, they give you tiny rewards which support beliefs around what you are capable of. So, don't wait, right in this moment program yourself with a future memory and test it out!

13

Information overload: Strategies for remembering

In this chapter you will learn:

▶ *increasing productivity and focusing on what's most 'important'*
▶ *remembering conversations on the fly*
▶ *techniques for filtering and remembering relevant information*
▶ *how to remember articles and latest news*
▶ *a process for remembering entire books*
▶ *how to rapidly capture details from meetings, presentations and conferences.*

Dealing with information overload is more than just increasing your capacity to remember. In a day-to-day sense it is more about filtering what is relevant, planning your time and prioritizing according to the value you or others will get. You will have high priority tasks to complete as well as information you want to learn and use in different areas of your life. This could be something that moves your business and career forward or something for your own personal development or that of your family. This is on top of the day-to-day stuff that comes up; emails from work and friends; social network updates; keeping up to date with the latest news; remembering facts from lectures, meetings or seminars; reading books and magazines on your favourite subject; or searching the endless amount of material available on the internet.

Case study: What am I committed to achieving today no matter what?

This one simple question has pretty much changed my life when it comes to creating focus and working on the most important task for that day which will build momentum towards my goals. While I was used to asking myself specific questions in the morning to direct my focus for the day, I picked this one up from a Brendan Burchard video.

It's now one of the first questions I ask myself in the morning in three key areas of my life – personal, relationships and professional.

Examples of answers to these types of questions could look like this:
* Personal: follow through on a new habit to drink more water
* Relationships: focus on becoming 'in the moment' when someone talks to me and things are busy
* Professional: Create a pitch deck for a new idea

While there will be other tasks which come up during the day, by having a very clear and simple focus about what is the most important things to achieve, my brain becomes primed to give these areas attention.

Try it now: Daily focus

* Ask yourself this question: 'What am I committed to achieving today no matter what?'
* Choose just one area of your life to relate it to – personal, relationships or professions
* At the end of the day run a quick review, without any judgement on how you did
* If your goal(s) were not achieved then look at what got in the way and come up with one thing you could have done differently
* If you succeeded then acknowledge your success, this could be as simple as smiling to yourself or punching the air!

You will find that by consistently asking yourself this question every morning you become aware of what is achievable, you are less stressed since there are less things on your mind and feel highly motivated as you are able to tick off the important things in your world each day.

Creative listening

The strategy of creative listening combines active listening and creative memorization; as a coach active listening is a key skill that you could break down into three component parts.

1 Practise listening on many different levels, what is the person saying? What might they be thinking? What might they be feeling? This is actually a lot harder than it may initially sound as for the most part people can spend a lot of time thinking about what 'they' want to say or how they will respond and will only be listening on a superficial level. With active listening you are at a much deeper level, completely focused in the moment.

2 Reflect, paraphrase and summarize what you hear or things you read. Depending on the type of conversation you won't always do all of these things. Reflecting is a technique where you play back what you thought someone said or did, this is great in a coaching conversation as it can raise a person's awareness, an example might be that someone says they are excited about a new role, however their tone and body language suggests they are stressed. By reflecting this

observation back to the client they can make a decision if this is the case. Reflecting can also be useful in negotiations (it's important when you use this technique that you have a good level of rapport). Paraphrasing what you hear is a great way of making sure you are really understanding the essence of what's being said and summarizing the key points can be used to confirm what's been agreed

3 Being a detective is all about asking questions. By taking on the persona of a Sherlock Holmes or Columbo and being genuinely curious about what a person needs you immediately listen on a much deeper level and you tend to get much higher engagement from the person who you are talking too.

Once you are listening on a deeper level you combine the iMind strategy (see Chapter 6) with either the chain method (see Chapter 5) or a memory network (see Chapter 6) to remember key facts, thoughts, feelings or actions that stand out. A simple way to practise this is to start by remembering just three things in some of the conversations that you have. As you hear the relevant information you create the images in front of you and either chain them together or put them on a memory network created on the fly. You can then simply look at your images to play back what you remember.

Case study: What did he say?

During a coaching session with a client who had challenges remembering key points in meetings, talks and conversations, we role played out the scenario where I was explaining details on a project that would be used to personalize a new digital product (this information was all new to him and creating digital products was not his domain). Whereas previously he would have found himself drifting off, thinking about other things and not grasping the concepts, after listening for about three minutes he was able to play back all of the key points I mentioned and more importantly understood what it was all about. He did this by employing creative listening.

Try it now: Remember conversations on the fly

If you are in any profession where you attend meetings, have conversations in the lift or by the cooler, or work with clients and customers, this technique is hugely valuable.

Where to start:
* In your next conversation, don't try to do everything at once, simply start by visualizing some key images that are sparked off in a conversation.
* As you start to become practised start to think about the other elements in creative listening, start small and grow your skill over time.

Emails and social media

Emails and social media can be a major contributor to information that comes our way. In the age of social media, information is also transferred across different mediums such as Twitter, Facebook and the ever growing Google+. With over 29 million users in the UK on Facebook at the time of writing and the way we consume information changing with mobile devices and tablets becoming the norm, the ability to access information anywhere adds to the opportunities available to us at any time. Creative memorization can play a role in supporting you with these media and adding value to what you can take away and use.

SETTING YOURSELF UP

It is a simple technique, but because of the nature of email and social media, with their addictive qualities, lots of people will find the urge to continually check if anything new has arrived, whether someone has replied to a previous email or post, whether there is anything important to respond to. At times this isn't a problem; however, during the course of a working day, depending on your career, you may find you receive a lot of emails, some that require direct action, some that require something to be remembered and others that are merely there for information purposes.

In order to set yourself up with an easier task, try chunking your day into times when you will respond to emails and times when you won't: morning, before lunch and late afternoon can work well. There might be a concern here that you will miss something 'important' but if it is important enough, it is more than likely to come to your attention. Avoid any other activity during these times, reprioritize, push back and stick to this rule. Let people know what you are doing so you can set their expectations and also give them an opportunity to contact you via other means if it has a higher priority. Depending on your career, setting yourself up in this way may not really be an issue, but if you find that emails or updates of any kind are getting in your way think about a similar model you can put in place that would help.

Try it now: Filtering and remembering

Once you have pre-allocated set times to work through email, build in time to memorize any relevant information and key actions:

- Start by following up on any email responses YOU are waiting on.
- Speed read your emails and any relevant documents attached, respond where necessary and flag any that require you to remember information or take any other action.
- Action all flagged email.
- For all the emails you have sent, capture the top three high priority ones that require someone to feed back to YOU.
- Repeat this cycle next time around.
- Avoid responding to email at any other time and let people you work with know that you are implementing this process, you'll be surprised at how many people want to do the same thing and follow suit.

By using this process you begin to free yourself from email addiction and start to take more control over your time and actions.

Documents and articles

Keeping up to date with knowledge and current research is what can give you 'the edge', getting you known as an expert in your field and a go-to person in your area.

Try it now: The article challenge

Time limit: 30 minutes

✼ Look for the key points in this article and use creative memorization to remember those facts: you can choose to use a memory network or the chain method or a combination.

Laughter leads to insight: Happy moods facilitate aha! moments

Stumped by a crossword puzzle? Try taking a break to watch a funny TV show. Recent research shows that people in a lighthearted mood more often have eureka moments of sudden inspiration.

Karuna Subramaniam, then at Northwestern University, and her colleagues found that boosting the mood of volunteers increased their likelihood of having an aha! moment that helped solve a word association puzzle. Those who watched a Robin Williams comedy special did measurably better at the task using insight than those who watched a quantum electronics talk or a scary movie. The games, in which players must find a word that connects three seemingly unrelated words, have been used for decades to demonstrate creative problem solving.

In the brain, sudden insight is accompanied by increased activity in the brain's anterior cingulated cortex (ACC) prior to solving each problem. The region is involved in regulating attention; in problem solving, it seems to work in conjunction with other brain areas either to stay focused on a particular strategy or to switch to a new one. Subramaniam found with functional MRI that people in a positive mood had more ACC activity going in to the task, which probably helped prepare the brain to find novel solutions. Participants who watched anxiety-producing movies such as The Shining, however, showed less activity in the ACC and less creativity in solving the puzzles.

Elizabeth King Humphrey

Scientific American Mind magazine, May 2011

✼ Create a mind map capturing your main thoughts (this was a rapid two-minute capturing stage).

✼ Colour in and decorate the map as you recite out loud in your own words.

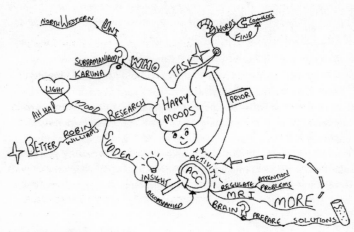

Figure 13.1 Mind map sketch.

News

Since news stories are more about what is happening now than what happened last month, last year or even last week, if you want to have the latest news logged in your memory bank, it is a quick and easy process.

Try it now: News headlines
Time limit: 15 minutes

* Create a memory network for the latest news stories and chunk into your favourite categories:
  ▷ World
  ▷ UK
  ▷ Politics
  ▷ Sport
  ▷ Entertainment
* You will probably only need ten nodes per chunk.

Whether you get your news from the TV, phone, computer or newspaper, while reading, listening or watching the news, do the following:

* Create a reference story for the relevant news article.

In the news today, 7 August 2011, there is a story of an aged Andy Warhol sculpture, depicting what he might have looked like had he still been alive. It was unveiled to mark his 83rd birthday.

* Speed read the article (if reading).
* Imagine the **statue** of **Andy Warhol** who once said, 'In the future everyone will be FaMous(83) for 15 minutes'.
* Dial up the intensity of this reference story so it becomes logged in your memory.
* Now decide whether you want to associate it with the latest news in your entertainment network; if so, connect Andy Warhol's statue to your first node.
* Once you fill up the nodes you have created in each category, simply erase the information on them and start again; you will find that with some news stories you will add more detail as they grow over time, for others they might only last a day as they become less relevant.

Books

Memorizing a book requires a combination of techniques; how much work you have to do depends on the level of detail you want from it. You have the option to use all or a subset of the strategies that are available to you in order to meet your purpose and put what you learn to use.

Having gone through the reading strategies chapter, you will know that the steps include:

▶ Create purpose and direction.

▶ Prime yourself through previewing.

▶ Capture the 10,000-foot view with a mind map.

▶ Speed read for comprehension and learning.

EIGHT-STEP STRATEGY FOR REMEMBERING ENTIRE BOOKS
With creative memorization there are four more steps (in bold type below) we can add to increase speed and retention. All of the following is done through the lens of the learning cycle – taking in sensory input, reflecting, abstracting and actioning.

▶ **Steps**

1 Create purpose and direction

2 Prime yourself through preview

3 Capture the 10,000-foot view with a mind map

4 **Construct your mental scaffolding, memorize relevant table of contents (TOC) and glossary terms**

5 Speed read for comprehension and learning

6 **Create detailed mind map of book**

7 **Memorize facts and details**

8 **Action it!**

▶ Once you know 'why' you are reading the book, you will have a clear purpose and direction. (2 minutes)

▶ Having a clear purpose will make it easier when you preview, priming your attention for relevant information that catches your eye. (5 minutes)

▶ Create your 10,000-foot view mind map; use this time to rapidly put your mind map in place and reflect on what you already know while you capture some initial questions. (10 minutes)

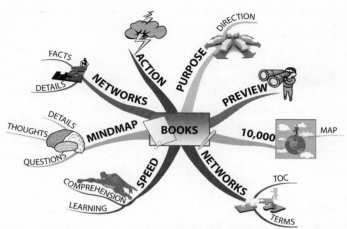

Figure 13.2 Steps mind map (created using ThinkBuzan'siMindMap http://www.thinkbuzan.com).

▶ Construct your mental scaffolding, decide how much of the book's table of contents (TOC) and terms in the glossary to memorize, depending on how familiar the material is. This may not always be necessary: a good rule of thumb is if it's a new topic, memorize at least some of the unfamiliar terms. Going through this process will set you up to speed read and allow you to mentally run through the book after you have read it, making more internal connections. (10 minutes– 1 hour, depending on complexity). *Limit yourself to an hour maximum for this phase.*

▶ Speed reading is where you will gain a deeper understanding of the material, reflecting on what you know internally and how it relates to other information you have had externally. It is important that you work on the strategies discussed in the speed reading section in order to avoid back-skipping, regression and subvocalization. (15 minutes–2 hours) *If it is over 2 hours take a break before continuing.*

▶ When your reading is complete, the initial memorization you did of the index can help in creating a detailed mind map. Aim to do this from memory and only refer back to the book when necessary. It doesn't matter if you make mistakes, you can cross-reference your mind map when you construct your memory network in the next phase. (15 minutes–2 hours)

▶ When your detailed mind map is in place, you can construct your memory network to remember any key facts and details. At this point you may need to refer back to the book (15 minutes–?). *The amount of time this takes will be dependent on your information.*

▶ The final essential step is to put what you have learned into action. This may take the form of a presentation or essay and, if it is a book that develops a skill, you put those skills into practice. Any action you take should be in keeping with your initial purpose. (Some books may not require all steps, it could be sufficient to set your purpose, preview, mind map and memorize some key facts – this could take as little as 30 minutes.

The amount of time you allocate will depend on your purpose and the level of detail you require. If you are doing a Masters degree, for example, there will be a much higher commitment of time; if you want to learn the latest project management skills from a new publication, your investment of time will be minimal.

Remember this

In the beginning this can 'seem' like a lot to do. In actual fact the time taken is minimal compared with simply reading a book and you will receive the major benefit of being able to retain information over a long period of time. My advice would be to run through this process with three books that interest you, play with it and adapt the model to your own style.

With some books you will need to take more 'action' in order to gain enough comprehension. A good example of this might be programming. By reading a book and memorizing syntax and concepts, you could get to a point where you understand what is going on; however, you wouldn't be able to pick up a laptop and start creating functions and classes. It is not enough to understand the concepts; in order to be a proficient or even basic programmer, you need to be 'writing code'.

You will be the best person to know the level of understanding you need in order to do your job. If you are studying anatomy for the purpose of qualifying as a pilates instructor, your depth of knowledge would not need to be at the same level as someone who is qualifying as a physiotherapist.

Try it now: Memorize a book
Time limit: 2 hours

It is time to put what you know into practice and pull together all of the strategies you have explored to date to memorize information from a book that is relevant to you and will help you achieve some purpose.

✽ For this exercise you should limit yourself to two hours and go as far as you can within that time. If this is your first attempt, be aware that it will take time for you to make this second nature.

✽ Use the eight-step process outlined to memorize a book of your choice; follow the steps closely and at the end think about how you can adapt them and improve them to fit your own style.

Example of how to set up and use your memory networks
Here is an example of how you may use the creative memorization part of the memorizing a book process. We will use a chapter from Essential NLP: Teach Yourself, *by Steve Bavister and Amanda Vickers (content used in this example is sourced from the 2010 edition of this publication). This book is a good example to use as it is a combination of understanding concepts, remembering what they mean and how to use them, and then rehearsing putting them into practice in a real-world situation.*

Let us imagine that we have set up a memory network to memorize the table of contents: we will pull out a chapter to look at on Framing. At this point we have no idea what framing means.

We will be using a memory network that is a mixture of locations and items within those locations as our nodes. Chapter 14 will be in the 14th location, let us say this is your living room. Within the living room we will create six nodes (these are the items in your living room: the first item might be the sofa, the second the TV, the third the fireplace and so on), one node for each section in that chapter.

Next memorize the sections in the chapter.

You glance through the glossary to prime yourself with one or two useful terms.

✳ *A frame is the boundaries or constraints of an event or experience (I don't need to put this on a memory network as I am just memorizing a definition; I will only need it when I think of it).*

✳ *Reframing is transforming the meaning of something by changing the context or frame of reference.*

The above steps will set you up for a good speed reading session.

After finishing, you create a mind map that is personal to you with your thoughts and questions.

Next you extract any relevant facts and details that make sense to store on a memory network: an example might be six-step reframing.

Bavister and Vickers talk about its use and how 'the "reframing" element involves separating the problematic behaviour from its positive intention, so that actions which on the surface appear to be negative are understood to have been trying to achieve something for the person'.

You would need to physically rehearse the six steps and then either create a chain of visual cues to remind you of the sequence of the steps or place the sequence of steps on a memory network.

You can continue this process of placing facts and details onto your memory networks or chains until you feel confident you have the required level of knowledge to fulfil your purpose.

When your memorization is complete you can move on to the final step: putting it into action.

Remembering books takes some effort and commitment; however, if you follow through, you can achieve some amazing results and each time you memorize a book you will find new ways of honing your skills.

Over the next four weeks, aim to practise these strategies on just one book a week. Start with a 'light' level of detail and, as you become more comfortable, build up the amount of facts and detail you consume.

Conferences

It is likely that at some point you will attend a lecture, a presentation, a seminar or a conference. When it comes to capturing, consuming, comprehending and remembering, the strategies you have learned throughout this book are invaluable.

Previously, while exploring mind mapping, you saw how these strategies could be used to capture relevant information, using where possible pre-structured templates to get you kick-started. It must be understood, however, that in certain situations, such as seminars and conferences, sometimes there isn't time to use colour and add lots of symbols, codes and images there and then.

If you attend a conference, the chances are that you will be going to many different talks during the time it is running, with huge amounts of information coming your way. It pays to have a strategy not only to capture and understand but also to memorize key facts and details.

Try it now: Techniques for lectures and seminars
Time limit: 10 minutes

Look at the following scenario and outline which of the techniques you have practised to this point would be beneficial while watching and listening to a lecture or seminar.

✱ One-day conference – you are attending a conference in which there are 11 talks you wish to hear; each talk lasts between 20 minutes and one hour. Some of the topics don't particularly interest you but since you are being sent there by your employer it is important that you pick up information.

Example
* *Define your purpose for the day, what you hope to take from it and what you will be able to offer others, e.g. your team, work colleagues, etc.*
* *Prior to going, memorize a list of talks that you are hoping to hear that will help you with your purpose.*
* *On the day, mind map all of your sessions. If you enjoy blogging, you can use the map as a reference for your blog and also upload the map for others.*
* *Consolidate the day onto one mind map; look for connections across all of your maps.*
* *Create a memory network for the event and memorize any 'key take aways' and speakers.*

Remember this

One of my experiences of how powerful mind maps are was at a conference called the Future of Web Apps. A speaker came on at the last minute as someone had dropped out; she had no slides and started giving a presentation on Operant Conditioning, comparing this with several websites. While mapping I was also reflecting on my own experiences and abstracting how I would apply this in the future.

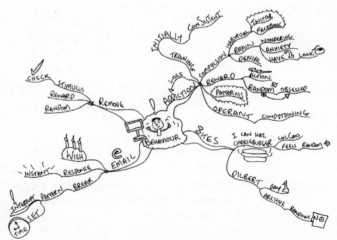

Figure 13.3 Rapid mind map from the Future of Web Apps Conference, 2008.

Focus points

* Use mind maps and creative memorization to help filter and remember important tasks. Pre-allocate time to deal with email and social media.
* Practise rapid mind mapping and the chain method to quickly consume and remember documents and articles.
* Keep up to date with the latest news stories utilizing categorized memory networks, speed reading articles and creating reference stories.
* Work with the eight-step strategy for remembering books – creating purpose and setting up your mental radar, previewing and capturing the 10,000-foot view, constructing your mental scaffolding and memorizing, speed reading for detail and comprehension, building your detailed map, creating deep knowledge through the use of memory networks and putting what you know into action.
* Decide on the level of detail you need to learn: for some needs a purpose, preview and mind map will be enough.
* Bring your skills to bear in meetings, seminars and conferences using rapid mind mapping.

Next steps

Gaining clarity on where your energy should flow, will not only make it easier to deal with information overload, it will empower you to enjoy it. By combining strategies that give you laser focus, prime you to filter what is important and help you remember, you will save time, feel more relaxed and be uber productive

Over the next week, after you wake up in the morning ask yourself this one question "What am I committed to achieving today no matter what?"

14

Delivering your message: Word for word

In this chapter you will learn:

- ► *how to design your visual cues*
- ► *how to get presentations in your body*
- ► *how to get it right, word for word.*

What's the story

Throughout this book we have seen how creating stories can be an invaluable technique in remembering, understanding and using information. The same is true when you are presenting information, performing scripts or thinking on your feet. At the core you have to take your audience on a journey, tell them the story in a way where they can reflect on it, relate it to their own experiences, question and formulate their points of view and ultimately provoke some type of action.

Key idea: Driving your story

The message and outcomes you want to deliver will drive your story. If it is a presentation for a new strategy, it might be an agreement on the way forward; if you are an actor in a play, it might be to have the audience experience a story from a different point of view. As you can imagine, whether you are presenting, acting out scripts or thinking on your feet, you can exploit the full spectrum of skills you are developing, particularly mind maps and creative memorization.

Case study: Do you fear public speaking?

In a 2014 article in the *Washington Post* about a survey run by Chapman University on America's biggest phobias, it might come as no surprise to some that public speaking came out on top at 25.3 per cent (https://www.washingtonpost.com/news/wonk/wp/2014/10/30/clowns-are-twice-as-scary-to-democrats-as-they-are-to-republicans/).

Having been lucky enough to do many talks over the years I'm always keen to help people improve in this area as when you get through that fear, it's very rewarding. In the mid-part of 2015 a client was recommended to me by Sarah Lloyd-Hughes, author of *How to be Brilliant at Public Speaking*. I had worked with Sarah previously as a guest speaker demonstrating how to remember presentations or speeches without the use of notes.

The client was Grace Quantok (gracequantock.com and healing-boxes.com) who was preparing for a TEDx talk. Grace had a number of memory challenges, including dissociative amnesia and cognitive dysfunction with short-term memory. I started working with her to see if any of the strategies I teach would be helpful. She had some strong beliefs about her memory not performing well, so I was keen to share a strategy that would produce an instant result and help start to shift some of those beliefs. In one of the first sessions we used a technique where you take each of the key points in your presentation and create an image to represent each of them.

Within one hour Grace had the whole structure of the speech in her head, more than that though, her confidence in being able to give this speech had also increased. It's probably fair to say she had a 'wow' moment. When it came to the TEDx talk she did something that previously she had a lot of anxiety over; she gave the whole speech with only a note card on her lap and afterwards realized she had only glanced at it a handful of times. It's a hugely inspiring and confident talk. You can see it here: https://www.youtube.com/watch?v=UN8_8q-KmdE

By learning to remember in a different way Grace broke down barriers not just about being able to give a speech but about what her own memory was capable of.

Presentations

There are whole books on the subject of giving engaging and valuable presentations. The goal here is not to focus on presentation technique but rather to give attention to how you can remember a presentation in such a way that you feel you can present it knowledgeably and with confidence.

Mind mapping is a powerful tool for brainstorming your ideas and crafting the message of your presentation; by following through on some of the techniques described in section on the four Cs (Chapter 8), you can construct engaging presentations that take your audience on a journey and leave them with something valuable.

Try it now: Presenting with a mind map

Time limit: 10 minutes

Spend no longer than five minutes creating a mind map of a 60-second presentation on a topic of your choice.

* Practise using the mind map as a guide as you give the presentation to a partner or friend, or simply standing up on your own.
* Capture your thoughts about what was challenging, what felt good and how you might improve.

Giving a presentation from a mind map is a technique in itself; committing a presentation to memory is taking it to the next level.

VISUAL CUES

Visual cues are basically images or reference stories, which you usually imagine within the location you are in at the time of memorizing.

Example

▶ *Use the iMind strategy*

▶ *Imagine that in front of you and to the left is a bicycle.*

▶ *Imagine that directly in front of you is a very creative painting.*

▶ *Imagine that in front of you and to the right is an old, large storybook.*

▶ *Look at each one of these visual cues and dial up the intensity.*

These visual cues represent three chapters in this book: the learning cycle, creative memorization and reference stories. The purpose of these visual cues would be to guide you through three topics in a presentation on *Improve Your Memory*.

You could create a normal memory network, but you tend to have to look internally for this; when you are thinking quickly, there is the potential to lose where you are. If the memory network is right in front of you, it is easy to keep track of where you are in the presentation, go off on a tangent and come right back to where you need to be. Ideally you would create a memory network in the place where you memorize the presentation and then create a similar network in the place where you will give the presentation. Details, facts or statistics connected to the presentation can be stored on any other memory network.

Key idea: Visual clues

There are many uses for visual cues: learning sports, games, dance, cooking, physical skills – you could think of them as physical cue cards. Once you have created your presentation, visual cues are your first step to memorizing the story you are going to tell.

BLOCKING

If you are an actor, dancer or singer reading this book, you will know what I mean when I use the term 'blocking'. It is nothing to do with martial arts or boxing. It is when you map out a general plan of where you will be on stage at a particular moment; in the same way, a mind map can give you a sense of the big picture – blocking a presentation or scene can give you this same big picture sense.

When working on a presentation that has some interaction with the audience, you would physically stand up, imagine you were in the location you will be presenting with the audience in front of you and 'block' out where you would want the audience member to be when you interacted with them. Blocking out a scene can make the words that you say more memorable as you are involving your procedural and episodic memory.

While blocking your presentation you should be referring to your visual cues, using them as a guide for what is coming next: this will also start to give you a sense of what might work.

ACT OUT!

Acting out a new presentation is essential if you want to be able to present with confidence, unless of course you are an old hand and it's something you do every day or have been doing for years. The idea of Act out! is that you give the presentation as if you were doing it for real; this means if you make a mistake you don't stop, you keep going. By acting it out you are able to experience closely how it will feel *in situ* and work out any pain points. You will also find out if any of your visual cues are flaky and need to be strengthened.

Act out! can be executed on two levels:

1 Exaggerated – here you exaggerate all your physical gestures, go completely over the top, do everything with intense energy and faster than you normally would, making sure that your diction is crystal clear.

2 Natural – this is how you will deliver it on the day, live, making sure you are connecting, being truthful, telling the story and delivering the message.

Try it now : How to remember anything
Time limit: 15 minutes

Put together a five-minute presentation on *Improve Your Memory*.
* Mind map your presentation. Include:
* a personal story you can share that will help people relate to your presentation
* an interaction (memory demonstration) you would like to happen during the presentation.
* Create a set of visual cues.
* Create a table like this for your notes:

Presentation	Visual cues

* Block the presentation.
* Act out! (exaggerated)
* Act out! (naturally)

Scripts and speeches

The techniques used for remembering presentations can also be used for remembering a script word for word: being clear on the story you are telling, visual cues, blocking and rehearsing are all valid.

The strategy that follows aims to demonstrate how you can memorize a script relatively quickly by devising a set of visual cues that act as a framework for the words to sit upon. Once these words are implicitly embedded in memory, there will be no need for the cues as you will 'know' the script, understand the meaning and be able to deliver the message confidently word for word.

Remember this

An actor will naturally use every part of the learning cycle, involving most if not all of their senses in the process of learning while creating emotion to experience and convey feelings. Most actors will have a method of working; there will usually be a basic framework depending on the medium. In theatre this might start with the script (sensory input); reflecting on the meaning and subtext, building a character, their thoughts, emotions, etc. (integration); questioning motivation, meaning, making choices with the director, making the director's choices fit, thinking about objectives, super-objectives and actions (integration); and finally actively testing their internal work. The purpose of this is not to try to teach you how to act but to take you through a strategy of learning scripts verbatim.

There are several other careers where being able to memorize verbatim is an essential skill: lawyers, police officers, politicians to name but a few. The strategy we will go through can be adapted, depending on your style and purpose.

PREPARATION

As well as being clear on the story and message you want to deliver, it can be useful to think about what sort of perceptions you want to evoke. An easy way in is to model your speech on someone who you believe would do it really well: how would they move? What sorts of intonation would they use? This gives you a quick way to get into the speech.

Try it now: Speak the speech, I pray you

Time limit: 30 minutes

Following on from the Shakespeare general knowledge theme, we will use part of this speech from *Hamlet* to demonstrate the steps you can go through when memorizing scripts verbatim.

Before you start memorizing, follow these steps to get to know the script:

1 Read it through it and gain a BIG PICTURE understanding of it.
  * What is the intention? Why are you saying this? Who is the message for?
  * What is the context? Where is the scene?
  * What are the emotions of the scene (keep it basic, happy, sad, angry, etc.)?
  * Mind map your thoughts.

2 Thinking about Step 1: Act out! (exaggerated)

HAMLET: Speak the speech, I pray you, as I pronounced it to you – trippingly on the tongue; but if you mouth it, as many of your players do, I had as lief the town-crier had spoke my lines.

Nor do not saw the air too much with your hand, thus, but use all gently; for in the very torrent, tempest, and as I may say the whirlwind of your passion, you must acquire and beget a temperance that may give it smoothness. O, it offends me to the soul to hear a robustious, periwig-pated fellow tear a passion to tatters, to very rags, to split the ears of the groundlings, who for the most part are capable of nothing but inexplicable dumb shows and noise. I would have such a fellow whipped for o'erdoing Termagant. It out-herods Herod. Pray you avoid it.

Memorize the script

1 Create a memory network with six nodes in your current location.
2 Create a set of visual cues (make the images strong, don't memorize words yet).
3 Connect the cues to the nodes on the memory network.

Script	Visual cues (examples)
Speak the speech, I pray you, as I pronounced it to you – trippingly on the tongue;	A speaking **speech** (script) with a big **tongue**
but if you mouth it, as many of your players do	A line of **players** opening and closing their big **mouths**
I had as lief the town-crier had spoke my lines.	I had a **leaf** stuck on a **town crier**
Nor do not saw the air too much with your hand, thus, but use all gently;	A hand with a **saw** in the **air** which comes down **gently**
for in the very torrent, tempest, and as I may say the whirlwind of your passion, you must acquire and beget a temperance that may give it smoothness.	A **torrent** of rain on a **tempest** who gets caught in a **whirlwind** of **passion**, **acquires** and **begets** a nun's outfit giving her **temperance**

Script	Visual cues (your cue)
O, it offends me to the soul to hear a robustious, periwig-pated fellow tear a passion to tatters, to very rags, to split the ears of the groundlings, who for the most part are capable of nothing but inexplicable dumb shows and noise. I would have such a fellow whipped for o'erdoing Termagant. It out-herods Herod. Pray you avoid it.	

4 See the visual cues and say the words aloud (connect the words to the imagery).

Consolidate

1 Block the scene.
2 Strengthen cues where needed (dial them up).
3 Act out! (exaggerate) at high speed.
4 Close your eyes, breathe deeply and let all the tension go from your body, as you start to relax. With your eyes closed, visualize the cues and whisper the script from beginning to end at speed.

Get it in your body

1 Act out! (exaggerated)
2 Act out! (naturally)

In the long term

1 Record yourself going through the speech.
2 Listen back while visualizing the visual cues and whispering the script.
3 Review after one hour, one day, one week, one month.

Remember this

Interestingly I always found as an actor that I didn't think of the words as much as I did the thoughts behind the words, what my objectives were, the intention and why I was saying the things I was saying. Another useful tip is once you have memorized the script, improvise around it or say the same words as a different character: this will all go towards making the words more memorable.

On the hoof

There might be times when you have to make a presentation with only a few minutes to prepare. If this is the case, the priority should be 'What is the story?', 'What is the message?', 'What is the key outcome?'. If you can quickly get a sense of these three things, then a few things ideas will come to mind that will help you construct an *ad hoc* presentation, or will at least give you a direction of travel.

You can also take the opportunity to find out what your audience (this could be anything from a few to many) wants to get from the presentation. Start whiteboarding a group mind map and memorize key thoughts you have as visual cues in the room, mentally constructing a presentation on the fly as you head towards the outcome you decided at the beginning.

Focus points

* Use a mind map to pull your presentation together and help craft the message of your story.
* Practise the technique of presenting with the aid of a mind map.
* Create and use visual cues, a way of constructing a live memory network right in front of you, guiding you in the right direction.
* Physically block your presentation and incorporate your procedural memory.
* Act out! helps to create confidence in your delivery and increases memory retention, first Act out! (exaggerated) then Act out! (naturally), making the experience as close to live as possible.
* Master the art of word-for-word scripts, build on your presentation techniques by dialling up your cues, Act out! at high speed and visualize the scene before performing with intensity.
* Be prepared to make an 'on the hoof' presentation, knowing your story, message and outcome and using a temporary memory network to capture the details.

Next steps

By giving yourself a framework for remembering presentations, talks and scripts, you are opening up a world of opportunities for your personal and business life. Having the confidence to have your voice heard is a very liberating experience.

How will being able to confidently deliver your message impact your life in the next six months? Identify three scenarios where you can experiment putting these skills into practice in the next seven days.

Part Four

Become an expert in your field

'Make your work to be in keeping with your purpose.'
Leonardo Da Vinci

15

Agile learning: The key to continuous development

In this chapter you will learn:

▶ *how to take control of your learning*
▶ *to create your learning roadmap*
▶ *an easy way to stay on target.*

The need to grow

The need to grow and learn is built into our DNA; knowing how to learn is an invaluable tool to have at your disposal and the strategies you have covered will set you up to do that. Knowing how to study is slightly different: study is more about planning and organizing, prioritizing, estimating how long things will take and creating rituals that help put you in a good state before you start.

Some will love studying while others will hate it; ongoing study, whether you think of it like this or not, is probably part of your everyday life. For some this is very structured, if you are a student, for example, or if you are training for a new career; for others studying happens here and there, keeping up to date with the latest trends in your area of knowledge.

Key idea: Strategy

By having a strategy for studying and learning, you can think about your development plan: what are the things that you need to study and learn in order to meet your goals, dreams or ambitions? If you could learn in exactly the way you wanted what would you achieve six months from now?

Try it now: How do you study and learn?
Time limit: 5 minutes

What techniques and approaches do you currently use?
* Brainstorm for three minutes.
* Where could you improve?
* What areas of your life would benefit from further study?

Although there are many options, the method shared here is derived from a term known as 'Agile Software Development' used by many companies across the globe as a methodology for producing software, websites and applications.

Agile learning is essentially a framework that aids you in planning, prioritizing and actioning. It is geared towards continuous development and learning with a purpose. It offers a high-level view of what you need to learn to achieve your goals and is flexible enough to allow you to change that view if needed (that's the agile part). It facilitates simple planning, estimation and prioritizing of the things you need to learn that will benefit you the most.

Remember this

Although there doesn't seem to be a completely consistent view of what agile learning is, the term itself has been used for a number of years. Within the context of *Improve Your Memory*, I have used it to describe how you can use an approach similar to one that has worked in the software world for a number of years, to meeting your own learning and development goals

Agile learning: What's inside?

There are a few terms that it will be useful to become familiar with before we look into the details.

Agile learning	Agile learning (mind map)
• The learning roadmap (a high-level view of the subject or area you are increasing your expertise in) • The learning topics (your area broken down into topics) • Themes (grouping of stories sometimes across learning topics) • Stories (tasks or things to learn that add value) • Points (number given to a story to estimate its size relative to other stories) • A sprint (a 2-week timeboxed learning period) • Sprint plan (short planning session) • The sprint board (used to track progress of a sprint) • Review (review at end of sprint)	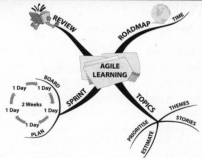 **Figure 15.1** Agile learning mind map (created using ThinkBuzan'siMindMap http://www.thinkbuzan.com).

LEARNING ROADMAP

Starting from the big picture view, your learning roadmap is a high-level view of how long it will take to complete your subject. It consists of a timeline and the **total estimated points** (this is the total points of all stories added together) it will take to complete your subject. When we go through estimating, you will see a useful way of working this out.

You can also reflect the learning topics on here. Your learning topics do not have to be studied in sequence, you will choose the highest-priority stories from across your subject for each sprint.

Learning roadmap	Size	Jan	Feb	Mar	Apr	May	Jun
Subject/Project: Become an executive coach	60pts					Sign up 10 clients	
Building a coaching business	20pts						
Executive coaching strategies	30pts						
Creating a web presence and attracting clients	10pts						

LEARNING TOPICS

The learning topic is a way of classifying your subject into vertical slices; themes are a way of grouping into horizontal slices.

Example

In the example below we have a subject or project that has four learning topics; topics 1, 3 and 4 also belong to the same theme. This is useful when you are prioritizing what needs to be worked on in the upcoming sprint. If a theme becomes really important, you can quickly look at the stories from each learning topic that have that particular theme and see which stories from those themes make sense to learn first.

If you are using software, you can create one mind map for your subject, individual branches for learning topics, theme branches from those topics and write your stories as 'notes' attached to the branch.

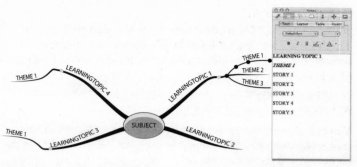

Figure 15.2 Subject mind map (created using ThinkBuzan's iMindMap http://www.thinkbuzan.com).

THE STORY

At the heart of agile learning is 'the story'. A story is basically a task, a thing to do. If, for example, you were studying to become a coach and you had to learn how to contract with a client, you would create a small story to represent that. You can write it in the way that works best for you.

Examples

▶ 'Learn how to contract with a client.'

▶ 'In order to offer value as a coach, I need to learn how to contract with a client.'

▶ 'I WANT to learn how to contract with a client, SO I can challenge them appropriately and give them value.'

Your stories will come from:

▶ Breaking your subject or project into learning topics.

▶ Writing your stories for each topic.

You can then:

▶ Group your stories into themes.

You can capture your stories in whichever way suits bests: it could be in a Word document or potentially on a mind map, as in the previous example.

ESTIMATING

Each story in your learning topic should be allocated a number to represent how 'big' you think it is; you are estimating, so it will never be totally accurate. We call that number – points.

A simple method of allocating points is to first prioritize your stories into the ones that are most important. Starting with the most important story and looking at the one below it, ask yourself, 'Is this story the same size, bigger or smaller?' Do this with each story and you will end up with a list of stories that go from very big to very small.

V. BIG		
BIG	BIG	BIG
MED		
SMALL	SMALL	
V. SMALL		

You then use a numbering system to represent your points (this can be whatever you like). This one works well: 1, 2, 3, 5, 8, 13, 20, 50.

Note: Anything over eight points is probably too big to be completed in a sprint.

Now you allocate points to the stories; the story at the bottom of the list gets a one:

8		
5	5	5
3		
2	2	
1		

If you have stories that are 13, 20 or 50 points, you will need to break them down into smaller stories just before you need to work with them in a sprint.

In order to figure out how long a learning topic will take to complete, you need to:

- Add up all the points from your stories within that learning topic.

- Work out how many points you can get through in a single sprint (you can guess or do one sprint and use that number).

- Take the total points in the learning topic and divide by how many points you can get through in a sprint (this will vary but you will have a ballpark figure).

Example

- *You have **20 stories** in **learning topic 1**.*

- *Let us say for demonstration purposes that each story is 2 points:*

- *2 points × 20 stories = **40 points** in total*

- *If you on average can complete **8 points** in a sprint (2 weeks), it will take you **5 sprints** (**10 weeks**) to complete learning topic 1.*

- *40 points in total / 8 points per sprint = **5 sprints***

- *5 sprints @ 2 weeks per sprint = **10 weeks***

Once you start putting points on your stories, this process becomes quite simple. In order for you to be able to create your learning roadmap, you will need to run a few sprints to figure out how many points on average you will get through in a sprint. Another option is to start by just taking a guess at how many point you will get through in a sprint and then adapt as you complete the first few sprints.

THE SPRINT

The sprint is a one or two-week study period (this is entirely up to you). It consists of three phases:

- **Planning the sprint** – this is a short 30-minute session in which you look at the stories across your subject and decide which ones are most important to be worked on.

- **The sprint** – the sprint will run over two weeks (usually five study sessions a week, you can decide). At the start of each session, you ask yourself three questions that will consolidate your current learning, prime your future learning and identify where you need to get help:

▷ What did I learn yesterday? (summarize it)

▷ What am I going to learn today? (summarize it)

▷ What are the major blockers or problems I need help with?

▶ **Sprint review** – at the end of the two-week session you:

▷ Review everything you have learned

▷ Consolidate your knowledge

▷ Identify any issues

▷ Decide if you need to create more stories.

THE SPRINT BOARD

Using a whiteboard is the simplest and easiest, low-tech way of planning your two-week sprints and making sure you are on target for your goals. The board summarizes:

▶ The **learning topic(s)** you are working on

▶ The **sprint number**

▶ The total **number of points** in your sprint (add up all **stories** to be completed)

▶ Major **themes** and **stories** in this learning topic

▶ A **pending** column for stories/tasks to be completed in this sprint

▶ An **in progress** column for what you are working on right now

▶ A **done** column for when your story is complete

▶ A **burn down** chart.

The burn down chart is a simple way of visualizing your progress during a sprint. Since each one of your stories/tasks has an estimated point size, you can create a graph that has points going vertically up the left-hand side and the days in your sprint going across the bottom. As you complete a story and move it to your Done column, you deduct that number of points and draw a line.

If you don't complete anything on Monday or Tuesday, but complete a story on Wednesday, your line will go straight across for the first two days and then burn down the appropriate number of points on Wednesday.

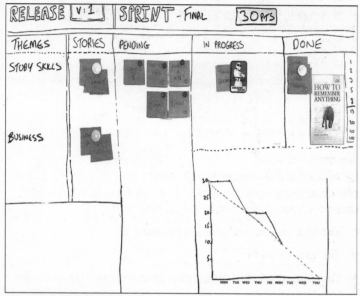

Figure 15.3 Sprint board.

Remember this

The sprint board shown above is actually the sprint board I used to deliver this book (the first edition); in this example I was both learning and completing a project.

Your ritual

After you have your planning set up and it comes to actually putting your skills into practice, you need to make sure you get the most out of the time when you actually capture and consume information.

When you think about how you have studied in the past, do you notice any behaviours that you repeated to get you into the swing of it? How you positioned your table or chair? Whether you changed the lighting in the room? Did you make yourself food and drink? Or maybe put on some music in the background? These types of repeated behaviours can help get a person into a specific state and create some focus.

You will see top athletes with these kinds of small ritual, a tennis player bouncing the ball a certain number of times or a long jumper running through the same physical movements and thoughts before powering forward.

If you become aware of your rituals, they can become a really useful tool to get you in a state where you are ready to study.

Try it now: Finding your ritual
Time limit: 10 minutes

To figure out what a good ritual would look like, it is useful to remember a time when you were in the zone, when learning felt easy. If you can't think of a time like that, then a time when you were enjoying reading a book (it might just have been for leisure).

* Breathe deeply and let yourself relax, become aware of your body in the chair, spend some time letting yourself fall into a relaxed state. When you are ready, close your eyes and remember a time when you were learning something that felt great; it may have been from a book or being shown a new skill by somebody. As you remember that time, imagine what your perfect study space would look like. What would you need to do to set up a space that made you feel relaxed, energized and focused, looking forward to developing your skills and knowledge? What are the things you would do and say to get yourself excited about learning the things that will make a difference to you in your life?
* Spend five minutes creating this space in your mind and creating the ritual that will get you into the state where you are excited to learn.
* Once you have finished, think about how you could create a similar space in the real world.
* Practise running through your ritual; practise getting into the zone so you are ready to learn.

Remember this

Whether you are learning or whether you are creating, a set of rituals to help get you into the right state is extremely useful. You will probably have experienced the scenario where you know you have to go and do something, perhaps write a report or learn something for a presentation or study for that exam, but you just didn't 'feel like it'. By creating rituals you can immediately change how you feel and get yourself to a place where you are ready to take action.

Case study: Training to be a Pilates instructor

Although the case study is focused on a specific career, the ideas and principles can be applied to any area, be it academic, technical or vocational.

Zoe was training to be a Pilates instructor. In order to achieve this goal the subject she studies required her to pass two exams:

* 1½ hour practical exam
  ▷ Client history, Postural analysis, Outline intended focal points, Warm up, Programme of exercises suited to client's needs
* 2 hour written exam
  ▷ 50–60 multiple choice questions covering anatomy, order of exercises, modifications to exercises with regard to postural type, muscle action during an exercise
  ▷ 6–9 longer essay questions

Zoe's learning topics

1 Skeletal system

2 Muscles groups and their range of movement

3 Anatomical terminology

4 Planes of movement & types of movement within the planes of movement

5 Types of muscular contraction

6 Neutral anatomical position

7 Postural analysis

8 Four types of postural alignment

9 Order of exercises – 34

10 Exercise cues and modifications

Zoe's themes

For some learning topics there will be themes – for example, **exercises** are a theme that cross over several learning topics:

Postural analysis (7) and Exercises cues and modifications (10)

What this means is that in order to know which **exercises** to give people, you need to understand **postural analysis**. This is the equivalent of using symbols on a mind map to represent a relationship.

Zoe's stories

Within the learning topics and themes, Zoe has created a set of stories that represent what she actually has to learn, remember and take action on.

Muscles groups and their range of movement (2)

Each muscle has an action (movements it creates), an origin (where the muscle begins) and insertion point (where the muscle ends).

* SHOULDER (a muscle group)
  ▷ deltoid
  ▷ pectoralis major
  ▷ coracobrachialis
  ▷ latissimusdorsi
  ▷ teres major
  ▷ rotator cuff
  ▷ tricepsbrachii
  ▷ bicepsbrachii

Zoe's story for this might simply say:

I WANT TO know which muscles produce which movements in the shoulder **SO I CAN** choose the right exercises to balance muscular issues for my clients.

Zoe will then estimate how big this feels using points: she thinks it's about 13, which probably means it might be too big to complete in a two-week sprint, with the other things she has to learn, so she breaks it down into smaller stories and keeps this one as a reference on a post-it note, which she sticks in the Stories column of her whiteboard.

I want to know the deltoid's action, insertion and origin (2 points). **I want to** know the pectoralis major's action, insertion and origin (2 points), etc.

Zoe now has the opportunity to bring all the resources she has acquired in creative memorization and put them into practice.

Remember this

Zoe managed to pass her exam with an average of 93%. Using creative memorization it took her only six weeks to memorize the information she needed for the written exam. I was particularly pleased and proud as she's my wife.

Having a strategy for studying can make a big difference, whether you are working through university, training for a new career or building your expertise within your area of business.

Case study: The focus board

Perhaps you are looking for something which feels a little bit more 'light weight' or are in a situation where you don't feel there is an overarching learning goal, however, you still want to build your skills in your area of expertise and be as productive as possible in your day-to-day work.

Over the past couple of years I have used a simple application called Trello and a three-column approach to managing time and growing skills based around business goals. Here is a snapshot of what it looks like at the time of writing this book. The three columns capture: four key projects, the WIP (work in progress) and a waiting column containing actions from other people which I need to follow up on. While I use Trello you could just as easily use pen and paper or Post-it Notes.

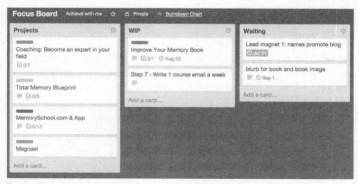

Figure 15.4

When you dig into the detail of improve your memory book this links through to a new board, which has a more granular view of each of the chapters that are either complete, being worked on or waiting to be started.

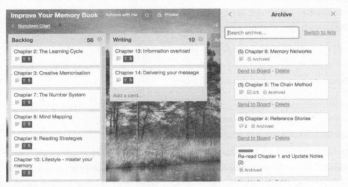

Figure 15.5

In order to understand how long it will take to complete the book, each of the chapters has estimate in points. Since Trello can plug into a burndown chart it's very easy to get a view as to whether or not I am on target:

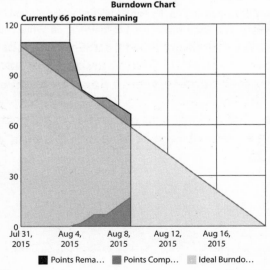

Figure 15.6

Focus points

✻ Agile learning is a framework that helps you plan your studying, prioritizing what needs to be done first, and provides a process for measuring whether you are on target.

✻ Agile learning is geared towards continuous development and learning with a purpose.

✻ The four big parts to agile learning are the learning roadmap, which gives a high-level view of timelines; learning topics, which are vertical slices of your subject and break down into themes and stories; the learning sprint board, which is your tool for keeping on track; and the sprint review, which happens at the end of every sprint.

✻ In agile learning, estimating is about working out the size of tasks relative to each other and estimating a point size that can be used to count up total points for a sprint, learning topic and subject.

✻ A sprint lasts for two weeks. Each day you should ask yourself:
  ▷ What did I learn yesterday? (summarize it)
  ▷ What am I going to learn today? (summarize it)
  ▷ What are the major blockers or problems I need help with?

✻ For effective study and a high level of performance discover your ritual.

Next steps

Start by thinking about what you want to achieve in the next six months? Give yourself 15 minutes to get clarity around this, note down or mind map a few of the key learning topics that will help you get there. This will set you off on the right path to becoming an expert in your area and bringing your goals to life.

16

In business

In this chapter you will learn:

- ▶ *what hard and soft skills you need to develop*
- ▶ *how to put your strategies into practice*
- ▶ *how to ace an interview.*

To make the best use of the techniques you have explored in this book, they need to be incorporated into how you operate and for that to happen you have to start by finding 'simple' ways in which you can use them that will give you a measurable benefit.

In this section we shall explore some ways that you can find that benefit and put into practice the knowledge you have accumulated thus far that can help enhance your effectiveness in a business environment.

The idea of this chapter is that it should stimulate your imagination to look for opportunities in your own life in which you can make the most of these powerful techniques.

Hard skills

In any role you will find there is a split between hard and soft skills. Hard skills may take the form of technical and academic knowledge: programming if you build websites or apps, sales strategies if you are in sales, medical knowledge if you are a doctor, business skills if you are a CEO of a startup, vocational skills if you work as a plumber, having a physically trained body if you are a dancer or athlete. These are all 'essential' skills in order to 'do' the role; in some of these professions you may start with basic knowledge and demonstrate lots of potential to learn and be trained on the job, in others you need to hit the ground running – this is usually an ongoing process for everyone.

Previously we have looked at how to remember specific 'things'. We are going to use some activities that will help you identify what are the hard skills and knowledge you may need to learn and remember in order to progress in your chosen career or area of business. This maybe in the area you are now or something which you aspire to do in the future.

Key idea: Strategies for hard skills

There is a clear application for the strategies in this book with regard to hard skills. The topics covered in previous chapters should give you a good understanding of how to remember technical, academic or practical skills that can improve your knowledge and application of that knowledge within your career, whether you are studying within education, training for a new role or building expertise within your current field.

Try it now: Identifying your 'hard skills'
Time limit: 10 minutes

Identify the hard skills you need to develop your domain knowledge to perform at your best within your career, if you are looking for a new opportunity, identify skills for your 'ideal career'.

✻ Create a mind map starting with a central image of your ideal career.
✻ Brainstorm branches of main areas of knowledge.
✻ Actively daydream switching between content and form.
✻ Capture the skills/knowledge you would need to work within this area.
Remember this is purely focusing on 'hard skills'. In the next chapter you can refer to this mind map when designing for your purpose.

Try it now: Where can your new skills help?
Time limit: 20 minutes

✻ Identify to 'what areas' you can apply creative memorization and the other strategies you have acquired to become efficient with these hard skills.
✻ On the previous mind map, identify branches where you could apply your skills (you may use a symbol for this – let's say a 'star').
✻ Add branches that summarize what you would need to do (create a memory network, mind maps on research, books to read, courses, etc.).
✻ Spend 15 minutes talking through the mind map aloud, making any alterations needed.

Soft skills

Soft skills are skills we all have to varying degrees; your ability to demonstrate these in interviews and in your role can have a big impact on the jobs you get and how you progress. In most jobs and careers there are consistent behaviours that employers are looking for; these are referred to as competencies. As you progress through your career, the expectation is that you will perform at higher levels of competency.

Case study: The value of soft skills

According to the British Chambers of Commerce workforce survey in July 2014, 88 per cent of businesses believe school leavers are unprepared for the world of work, in comparison to 54 per cent of businesses that thought graduates are unprepared for the workplace. They suggest that there is a need for stronger links between educators (schools, colleges and universities) and business to better prepare young people for work.

Out of the 3,000 companies survived, over 57 per cent though young people lacked basic 'soft' skills, such as communication and team working, to succeed in the working world.

The ability to communicate, work well in a team, be resilient and lead are skills not just required by students and graduates, they are skills that play a large part in pretty much any role you embark on.

At the EQ summit in London, exploring the importance of emotional intelligence in business, Sky CEO Jeremy Darroch was quoted as saying, 'A lot of the old skills of leadership aren't fit for the future. The idea that I can sit in the corner office and call the shots is long gone. Empathy is now the single most important skill when you get to the top of an organization. It means you can frame opportunity and challenge in the right way.'

In an interview with Anthony Gell, Daniel Goleman, talks about how the best leaders are not those with the best 'hard' skills but soft skills. If a leader in a team is in an upbeat mood and can manage their own state, then people in that group catch that mood and performance goes up, decision-making gets better and creativity improves.

COMPETENCIES
The following is an example of competencies that shows a set of 'guidelines' around the types of behaviour to expect from two

different soft skills. Each soft skill has three different levels – 1 is Good, 2 is Very good and 3 is Excellent.

Try it now: Memorizing your competency
Time limit: 5 minutes

The table below is just a template and the behaviours may not be the same at your place of work; they will most likely have their own definitions and levels.

By memorizing the competencies and the different levels you can gauge which level you are performing at.

Communication	Reference stories (your stories)
Level 1	
Clear and concise	
Presents point of view to colleagues	
Pro-active communication	
Level 2	
Range of techniques to influence	
Adapts to situations	
Delivers hard messages well	
Level 3	
Empathizes in difficult situations	
Skilful negotiation techniques	
Adapts to wide range of situations	

Creative thinking	Reference stories (your stories)
Level 1	
Simplifies problems	
Identifies key information to support decision	
Level 2	
Simplifies complex problems	
Gathers information and distils quickly	
Creative in solving problems	
Level 3	
Thinks strategically	
Aware of the Big Picture	
Facilitates effective problem solving	

Other competencies include things such as teamwork, leadership, negotiation, flexibility, etc.

Scenarios

Now you have a good understanding of what 'high levels of competencies' look like, you can start to explore how the strategies you have learned to date can be applied in various scenarios.

For each one of these scenarios, you should think about which competencies apply and what level you would need to perform at in order to be successful.

This is by no means a full picture of how the strategies you have learned can be applied to a business scenario, it is simply some snapshots that should inspire you to look at your current and any future roles and seed ideas of how you might employ them in your own world.

MEETINGS

Whether you are with clients, in the boardroom or in the coffee shop, meetings are part of a lot of people's lives in many careers. As much as information overload, there can be meeting overload. In a meeting situation you can use the learning cycle, creative memorization, reading strategies and mind mapping to your advantage.

Try it now: Meetings for business
Time limit: 15 minutes

Play out each meeting scenario, identifying the actions you would take to help you be more effective.

The scenario: Off-the-cuff meetings

You meet someone outside a lift, you don't have anything to take notes on or it may not be appropriate (or you might be having a coffee, lunch, etc.), they tell you five bits of information that are relevant to you, maybe about the project they are working on. They also mention a person who it might be useful for you to meet. During the conversation they remember a presentation you showed them a while back and ask if you can email it to them.

Information:
* Interested in booking a one-to-one session 30 January
* They mention an article about memory by Joshua Foer
* They are taking their pilot's licence, need help studying
* Belief about having a notoriously bad memory
* Two kids named Jill and Max
* John Stanton is the person who has been asking about a different type of event for his team
* Would like the 30-minute presentation he saw that I ran about six weeks ago.

In practice
* What strategies could you apply to this scenario?
* What competencies come into play and what level do you need to perform at?
* Use the information in the scenario to practise this example.

Strategy examples
* *Have a set of pre-prepared memory networks available: you may have about ten of these with 20 nodes/files on each one – you will use these for random information that you receive at a time where you wouldn't be in a position to take notes. You will store the key information you hear on your memory network during the conversation, using the techniques you have learned. For each bit of information, you create your image and associate it to your node/file.*
* *Memorize the first five key pieces of information you hear while having a conversation with a colleague, the person's name you want to meet and the presentation you need to email them.*
* *Alternatively, you can create a memory network on the spot using the items around you: this can be very effective, essentially setting up some visual cues. If you are having a conversation beside a lift, start with 'items' that are on your left and cast your eyes around in a clockwise*

*direction, picking out key items to act as your nodes/files – you can even
use different parts of the body of the person you are talking to. Again,
for each bit of information, you create your image and associate it to
your node/file.*

The scenario: Meetings with an agenda

You have been invited to a meeting in about one hour's time: there are
only two invitees' names that you recognize, you have never seen the
other names before, although you have an idea of which team they are in
and their role. The agenda is focused on a topic that is important to you;
there is some information you are unsure of. You will need to prepare
for the meeting (taking into consideration 'a new way of thinking'). It's
important that you get agreement on one of your ideas; you know that
one of the people in the room will have an opposing point of view. When
you get into the meeting, there are ten people there. Introductions are
made and the meeting begins.

In practice

* What strategies could you apply to this scenario?
* What competencies come into play and what level do you need to
  perform at?
* Think of an upcoming meeting.
* Go through the steps in the strategy example or use strategies of your
  own you have identified.

Strategy examples

* *Prepare for your meeting by mind mapping out the agenda, the
  outcomes (both yours and others), the facts that you know, areas you
  don't know (research these if time, or identify appropriate questions
  and responses), map out how you 'feel' and how others might 'feel',
  map out the risks and benefits associated with ideas (identifying 'who'
  benefits), where there is an opportunity to focus on interests between
  people in the room, and where there is conflict, map out potential
  options you could put on the table. What would your ideal outcome
  look like? You can use this map in the meeting as a reference, make sure
  you talk through the meaning of each branch out loud, or even share it
  with a colleague on your team to get some feedback – if you have time,
  you may want to create an edited version for the meeting itself.*

* Research information you were able to identify and add to your map.
* Create a memory network or use one you built before and store any key facts you would like to keep in your head.
* It can be useful to memorize your ideal outcome and any facts or details associated with it.
* Look at the names on the agenda and spend a few minutes creating images for their names so you don't have to do this in the meeting – if their photos are in a system somewhere, look them up so you know who they are when you see them.
* Once in the meeting, memorize the names of the people around the table, try to do this just before it starts, so you can recap if you go around the table; this will also help build some rapport with the people you don't know and perhaps get some early insights.
* Make sure there are clear agreed outcomes at the beginning of the meeting.
* Having a pre-prepared mind map with a branch for the agenda and branches for questions, challenges, interests, ideas, solutions, agreed, outstanding and thoughts will allow you to capture 'key' information throughout the meeting. It is all right for people in the room to see these notes and can be helpful when putting your point of view forward as you can share your thinking visually on the mind map – capturing more issues, ideas and offering potential solutions.
* If there is information that is relevant but that you don't feel comfortable putting on your mind map but would like to reference later in the conversation, simply store it as a key fact on your pre-prepared memory network.
* Use your mind map to play back what was agreed (where needed) and what is outstanding, with follow-up actions and criteria for their success.
* At the end of the meeting, you can memorize any key outcomes on your pre-prepared memory network that you can reference at a later date.

Remember this

When you practise this in a real situation it is useful when you create the association to ask a question about it and reflect the information back. This benefits you in two ways: first, it gives you more time to create the associations, and second, you confirm the information is correct. When you hear 30 January, imagine a MaCe (30) being swung around by a bottle of GIN (Jan) – you quickly associate that to a nearby file and ask a question, e.g. 'So on 30 January, what is the most important thing you would like to take away from this?' While they search for the information, you reaffirm your association; they will then give you some more key information – passing their pilot's exam, etc. By listening, reflecting, abstracting, asking questions and playing the information back, you are using the learning cycle to lock the information in your mind.

Key idea: Emotional intelligence

A key skill when influencing is being able to separate the people from the problem, using your own emotional intelligence to understand the needs of others. By mind mapping, capturing potential feelings and hard facts, you can remain subjective and non-judgemental, making sure that you maintain rapport while being hard on the problem you are looking for a solution to.

If you spend some time on creating this ritual when preparing for meetings, you will find it takes very little time and you can hone it down into four to five minutes when needed. It will allow you to be the most effective you can be, prepared and also able to improvise when needed, and setting yourself up a framework to retain key facts that will be useful to you at a later date.

BRAINSTORMING

Whatever career you are in, at some point you will have to come up with ideas or solutions to problems, perhaps even on a daily basis.

From Edward De Bono's six 'thinking hats', we have a great model in which to utilize mind mapping in many situations and with varying numbers of people. Six thinking hats is a metaphor that allows a group of people to approach a situation or problem from the same perspective.

From a very high-level summary, a group of however many people take a specific topic or challenge and metaphorically wear the same hat; by stating which hat the group is wearing, the group can approach the challenge from the same perspective: 'Right, let's wear the white hat – everyone focus on the facts, the information we know.'

There are six different coloured hats:

▶ **Blue** – controls the direction of travel and focus, sets the outcomes and summarizes conclusions – one person generally wears this hat, although it can be passed around.

▶ **White** – used to gather information.

▶ **Red** – used to express feelings, both positive and negative (there is no justification needed with this hat).

▶ **Yellow** – looks for the value in the challenge.

▶ **Black** – critical (not emotional but logical and assesses negative aspects).

▶ **Green** – drives new ideas, provokes alternatives and helps to form solutions.

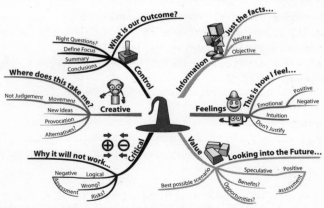

Figure 16.1 Mind map of the six thinking hats (created using ThinkBuzan'siMindMap http://www.thinkbuzan.com).

Try this now: Brainstorm for business

Time limit: 15 minutes

Although this is aimed at a group, you can practise it on your own. Play out the following brainstorm scenario, identifying the actions you would take to help you be more effective.

The scenario

You are with a group of colleagues working through a specific problem or challenge to do with your current job. There are different points of view in the room; however, it is important that you get to a conclusion in the next 60 minutes.

In practice

❋ What strategies could you apply to this scenario?

❋ What competencies come into play and what level do you need to perform at?

❋ Even though this is aimed at a group, it can work just as well on your own. Choose a problem or challenge you have and run through using the strategy examples or your own approach.

Strategy examples

❋ *Whether you take a thinking hats approach or use something a bit more free flow, mind mapping can be an excellent way of brainstorming with a group of people.*

❋ *Either lead the mind mapping brainstorm and draw on a whiteboard, or use an application such as iMindMap or Mind Manager.*

❋ *Or break the group into smaller numbers of two or three to do the initial brainstorm.*

❋ *Use a technique such as thinking hats to consolidate the group's ideas and come up with a solution.*

❋ *Pre-prepare a memory network or use the room that you are in and create one on the fly.*

❋ *Throughout the session and at the end memorize the outcomes or use your mind map as a tool to memorize the information after the brainstorming session — make sure you set time aside afterwards to do this.*

PRODUCTS

If you are a product manager, CEO or entrepreneur, there are many different applications for the techniques you have experienced so far in relation to bringing a new product to market.

To inspire your thinking in this area, consider some of the various elements that are involved when delivering a new product: your customer segments, early adopter problems, potential solutions, competitor research, KPIs, the vision and USP, unfair advantage, channels to market, cost, revenue etc.

You then have the logistic of bringing something to life in terms of a roadmap, backlog of features, experiments to run, dependencies and risks. If this is the area you play in, let your mind think about where you might apply the learning cycle, creative memorization and some of the many strategies in this book to improve your performance and productivity.

Try this now: Your product
Time limit: 30 minutes

Play out any of the following scenarios that you can relate too (even if you can't just give it a go and see what happens), identifying the actions you would take. There are many other areas that could benefit from applying the strategies you have learned. The purpose here is to identify some quick, easy wins that you can put into practice, in your own projects.

The scenario

You are leading a new product which is at the product/market fit stage and are trying to understand if the product you are creating is actually going to solve some key problems of your target audience.

In practice
* What strategies could you apply to this scenario?
* What competencies come into play and what level do you need to perform at?

LEADERSHIP

The topic of leadership is vast; in order to start to explore the application of your strategy toolkit, we can look at a small slice. From a general point of view, in order to lead, you have to be able to influence, whether that is with your peers or leading a team. In order to influence someone, you have to know already what influences them (*Creating Lasting Change*, Robbins). What are they all about, what are their beliefs, what drives them, what makes them tick? Try to understand their world and not judge it. Once you understand, you have a bigger chance of influencing and leading them to demonstrate behaviours found in a high-performing team.

In Ken Blanchard's *One Minute Manager* book, *Building High Performing Teams* (Blanchard, Carew, Parisi-Carew, 2004), he refers to the PERFORM mnemonic, in order to paint a picture of what such a team would look like:

▶ P – Purpose

▶ E – Empowerment

▶ R – Relationship

▶ F – Flexibility

- ▶ O – Optimal performance
- ▶ R – Recognition
- ▶ M – Morale

The idea is that each of these words has a set of characteristics that describe what a team would be demonstrating if they were performing at a high level. Purpose, for example, is having a common view, understanding what the vision is and why, seeing clear ways of achieving objectives.

By leading a team to meet those behaviours, you work towards creating a team that is driven, engaged and responsible for making things happen. The output of this is they strive to deliver on time and to the required specification and have a strong focus on the quality of their work and the contribution this makes to the bigger picture. Within this picture, it's also a fun place to be.

If you are currently in a team, or leading a team, think about what a high-performing team looks like for you. On a scale of 1–10, where does the team currently sit?

Try it now: Objectives for leadership
Time limit: 15 minutes

Play out this scenario, thinking about any experience you have had at leading or influencing people: what was your approach? What worked well and what could you have done better?

The scenario

You are fairly new to a team you have been tasked to lead. The team has gone through a lot of change and even though there are now some good opportunities on the horizon, its purpose and responsibilities are unclear, communication could be better and morale is quite low.

In practice
* ✳ What strategies could you apply to this scenario?
* ✳ What competencies come into play and what level do you need to perform at?

Interviews

Mostly everyone at some point will be involved in an interview process. With interviews there can be a great deal of anxiety and stress; in order to reduce these to a minimal level, being secure in your knowledge and your ability to demonstrate that knowledge is essential. Using your memory strategies, there are some quick wins you can put into practice that will ensure you can perform at your absolute best in an interview situation.

Try it now: Demonstrating high levels of competencies

Time limit: 15 minutes

Your plan for demonstrating high levels of competencies: reflecting on the previous examples, identify where you can put your skills into practice and what you will gain from that.

The scenario

You are interviewing for a new role in an area that you are excited and passionate about. You have been asked to demonstrate fully the skills and knowledge required for the role.

In practice
* What strategies could you apply to this scenario?
* What competencies come into play and what level do you need to perform at?

Strategy examples
* *Use relaxation and visualization techniques to 'pre-rehearse' the interview in your mind as if it is happening at that very moment, feeling relaxed and enjoying sharing your skills and abilities.*
* *Apply reading strategies to research valuable information about the company you are aiming to work for.*
* *Mind map information about the company, interviewers, your outcomes, stories that demonstrate your hard and soft skills, questions, why you want the job, why you should get it.*
* *Create memory networks to store the essential facts.*
* *Memorize stories that demonstrate your skills working through strategies in 'delivering your message'.*
* *In the interview, memorize the names of the interviewers.*
* *In the interview, have a pre-prepared memory network to capture any useful facts you may want to question later.*

There are almost endless uses for these strategies with regard to soft skills: the above five areas are just a small taster. In the next chapter you will bring together the ideas throughout this book and abstract your own view about them and focus on what benefits they can bring to your own career.

Focus points

✱ Identify what competency levels you are currently performing at and what you need to do to improve.

✱ Capture times that you are demonstrating a high level of competency and add them to a mind map or memory network.

✱ Practise using memory networks for off-the-cuff meetings and remembering details; you can also make on-the-spot visual cues.

✱ Use mind maps and creative memorization to prepare for meetings, memorizing agenda, facts and your outcomes. Memorize names during the meeting and any key facts, using a mind map to capture, reflect what has been said and summarize.

✱ Play with DeBono's six thinking hats and have dynamic brainstorming sessions.

✱ Use mind maps to plan deliverables, dependencies and risks combined with creative memorization to remember your vision and pitches.

✱ If you lead a team, think about PERFORM and how you can bring your skills to bear to facilitate a high-performing team.

✱ Be confident at interview, knowing that you have memorized key facts, competencies and stories.

Next steps

Continue to build your own awareness of your hard and soft skills, where you perform well and how you can improve using the range of strategies you now have at hand. While there are lots of techniques you can apply, one of the easiest things you can do is have a simple thought in your mind, "what is the one single thing I can do to perform to my best in this situation?"

17

Your strategy: Design for your purpose

In this chapter you will learn:

▶ *how to identify your talents and purpose*
▶ *how to GROW your potential*
▶ *to condition a mindset to achieve your goals.*

There are many ways in which you can scope out your goals and strategy for success. In this chapter we will look at some of those options. Each section of this book has built the breadth and depth of your knowledge and given key insights and practical examples of how thinking in this way and applying it in your life can bring real demonstrable benefits. This chapter will focus specifically on how the strategies you have explored can help you build expertise in your field to progress your career or business and find the best fit with your purpose.

How do you currently think of your career or business? Is it a job? Your work? Your mission? Your passion? How you refer to this area of your life will have an impact on what it means to you and how you approach it.

Your purpose

In order to understand your purpose, it can be useful to think about your natural talents. Perhaps you have a natural talent to empathize, build relationships, persuade or inspire. Maybe you are driven to contribute to others, paint the big picture or be physical. It could be you are naturally gifted at forming objectives, organizing, making sense of problems or have a bond with numbers and patterns.

If you feel your current role is not in keeping with your purpose, it doesn't necessarily mean that you should jump ship. By working out what you are inherently good at, what your natural talents are, you can become clearer about your purpose and how that can help you add value to anything that you do as you work towards your ideal role.

Try it now: Identifying your talents and purpose
Time limit: 5 minutes

Ask yourself the following questions, creating a mind map to capture and elaborate on your thoughts. Your outcome should be to identify the things you are naturally good at (your talents) and use that to feed ideas around your purpose and where you can really add value in your personal life and your career.

* Where do you feel you have been successful in the past?
* What are the things you most enjoy?
* What are you naturally good at?
* What do you love to do?
* Where do you believe your natural talents lie?
* How can you bring your talents to bear in your current role?
* In which role do you believe you would add the most value?
* What do you think your purpose is at work or in your business?
* What do you think your purpose is in life? (If you don't know, pretend you do and think about what could it be.)

Case study: Finding your talent

In the 1990s, I worked in a theatre bar. The early few days were not great, I wanted to be on stage rather than serving behind the bar. I knew I had to make a change as I needed the job, so I thought about what I could bring to the role. What was I good at that would help me in this situation? It was clear to me that one of my talents had always been my ability to relate to people. My purpose became *to use that talent to create a positive change* in the people I served and my co-workers. As a by-product, I became a pretty good barman, memorizing customers' names and drink orders, quick at serving and creating games with the team about getting tips. This didn't stop me from looking for my ideal role, in fact it motivated me more to find a job that was a better fit and within ten months I was on the West End stage (in the same theatre). This purpose has remained at the core of everything I do, from actor to product guy to coach.

Try it now: Your ideal role!
Time limit: 5 minutes

Thinking about your talents and purpose, ask yourself this next set of questions to identify where they would best be put to use. Create a mind map to capture and abstract your own thoughts.
* What are the roles you believe you can do now, at some point in the future or would have loved to do as a child?
* What is the best fit for your talents and purpose?

* Pick out your top choice. Why does this stand out for you?
* Who would you be working with?
* Where is your ideal location?
* When could you imagine yourself being in this situation? (If you can't, imagine yourself 3–5 years in the future and see the scene clearly in your mind.)
* Mind map this 'ideal scene'.

The strategy

If you have a picture of your purpose and your ideal role, you can start to look at how to make that role a reality and how your creative resources can help you get there and add real value to your everyday life.

Learn how to GROW

The GROW model was created by John Whitemore back in the 1980s. On the outside GROW looks like a fairly simple framework and in some senses it is. While there are many complexities that lie beneath, it is simple to get started and start seeing immediate results.

As the word might suggest, one of the benefits of using GROW is to grow your own potential, overcome challenges that come up in your life or career and take the desired actions to achieve your goals. Let's take a look at each of areas:

G stands for Goal: A poorly imagined goal has the capability to divert, frustrate and even disillusion a person, while a strong goal has the power to inspire, motivate, direct and deliver purpose.

The good news is, you don't have to be a brilliant word-smith or spend days, weeks or months crafting a brilliant goal. All you have to do, is be able to imagine a future outcome in your mind. This is well within your capabilities with the strategies you have practised in this book.

R stands for Reality: When faced with a goal the reality of where you are 'today' can feel overwhelming and it can be all too easy giving your focus to all the reasons why something 'wont" happen. The strategy here is to realize, acknowledge and accept the reality of where you are today and the challenges you might face so you can develop some options to overcome them should you need to.

O stands for Options: like a game of chess, being able to predict potential outcomes and have more than a couple of options to deal with challenges not only sets you up to be prepared with a practical list of actions, it also brings a feeling of certainty about success. This in turn can help to shift beliefs about what you are capable of and foster resilience when things don't go as planned. The key with options is to go beyond the number you think you need. Use 'what if' questions to generate scenarios that could happen. For each 'what if' come up with a solution. When you think you have done all you can, search for more by asking yourself, 'What would never happen?' this will help your brain come up with some extra scenarios you can create solutions for.

W stands for Will: what 'will' you do next? Once you have clarity on your goals and the benefits they will bring, the things that can slow you down or get in your way, a wide array of options, it's time to nail down the first set of actions. What are the 1–3 top things you 'will' do in the next day to a week? How committed are you to doing these things on a scale of 1–10? How confident are you that you can achieve what you are setting out to do? When you run a scaling exercise like this you want to be at an 8 or above. If you find that your confidence levels are at a 5, then either change your actions or ask yourself, 'What would need to happen for me to be at an 8?'

Remember this

The GROW model may affect two different types of change: Transactional and Transformational. The first refers to the types of change that may lead to an outcome based on a set of steps of a plan, a solution to a problem, a resolution to a key decision. The second refers to the type of change that may bring a new belief about what you are capable of, what you feel is important to you in terms of the values you experience (security, freedom, variety, contribution, growth etc) or how you feel about yourself in relation to your self-esteem and confidence.

Try this now: Learn how to GROW
Time limit: 10 minutes

Think of an area of your life you would like to change in a positive way. Be as specific as possible: a new skill you want to master, a promotion, feeling differently about a relationship. Now try running through the GROW model for yourself by answering the following questions:

* What is your Goal?
  ▷ If you could have things just the way you want them what would that look like to you?
  ▷ Make the experience as vivid as possible, like creative memorization, use all of your senses and emotion as you construct this 'future memory'.
* What's the reality?
  ▷ Identify the key challenges that will slow you down or block you
* Generate 10 options
  ▷ Go beyond just 2 or 3 things you could do to help you achieve this goal
* What will you do next, how will you do it and when will you do it?
  ▷ Identify how committed you are on a scale of 1–10
  ▷ Identify how confident you are on a scale of 1–10
  ▷ If you are below an 8 on either, ask yourself, 'What needs to happen for me to be at an 8 or above?'

The goals you create don't necessarily have to be life changing. You can apply the GROW model to what you would like to achieve from reading a book, going to an event or a particular meeting you are having that day. For the latter, your goal could be to get agreement on a new idea. Prior to the meeting you would identify the reality of the challenges you may face; generate options to facilitate a successful outcome and have a specific approach to what you will do next.

Mindset

One of the last elements to consider once you understand your purpose, have defined your ideal role and have created a plan with the GROW model is to create the beliefs that support and help you generate momentum.

In *The Body You Deserve*, Anthony Robbins gives a metaphor for beliefs, comparing them to a table top: for this table top to have any substance it must have legs to hold it up; these legs are references, memories that support this belief.

► If you believe that you have a bad memory – this belief is probably held up and supported by a series of past experiences; perhaps you couldn't remember facts at school, or were always forgetting names.

► If on the other hand you believe, not just mentally but at your core, that you have a great memory, this belief will support you in your actions and your ability to remember, as well as drive you forward to achieve your ideal role.

By actively participating in *Improve Your Memory*, you will have had a concrete experience, creating new references. You will have learned ways of remembering things you might have thought impossible in the past, forming new neuronal networks and a belief that now says, 'I have a great memory.'

Try it now: Shift your beliefs?
Time limit: 10 minutes

Think about your goals and identify as many beliefs you have that could slow you down, hold you back or get in your way. Once you have this list, for each of those beliefs create a new empowering belief to replace it. For example:
* Current belief: I don't believe I have the time to make this happen
* New belief: I have all the time I need when I direct my focus and energy
Once you have your list of new beliefs:
* Create a memory network and memorize each of those new beliefs
* Each morning for the next seven days review and experience those beliefs.

By running through this short daily activity you are priming your brain to give focus and energy to these new set of empowering beliefs. This in turn will affect your decisions, actions and help build momentum towards your goals.

Try it now: Where are you now?
Time limit: 5 minutes

In the earlier sections of the book you rated your memory on a scale of 1–10 on where you were then and where you would like to be.

Where would you put yourself on that scale now?

You also benchmarked your core creative memorization skills on a scale of 1–10:
* Relaxation
* Concentration
* Imagination
* Association
How would you scale your creative memorization skills now?

Final thoughts

Your ability to remember anything is almost limitless. You can choose to train your memory to perform at the highest of levels, or you can choose a few simple techniques that you enjoy and add some value to the things you do.

There have been a number of techniques and strategies explored throughout this book. I wanted to share with you my view of a simple picture of how it all comes together.

Everything should be done through the lens of the learning cycle: make yourself open to sensory input, make sure you reflect on the information and relate it to something you already know, look for ways to make the information your own, question it and think how it fits in with your purpose and take some form of physical action. Create as many connections as you can to the new information.

Mind mapping and reading strategies give you the big picture and the detail, employing whole-brain strategies that prime you for relevant information and make the relevant information understandable, memorable and easy to communicate.

Creative memorization is the ace in the hole, natural strategies that make the most of how you create memories. Wielding this skill will allow you to consume huge amounts of detail and facts, and create frameworks that act as the scaffolding for new information to be built on.

All these strategies combined with a plan of where they will add real value can create lasting change in your life, your career and your business.

Use what you've learned and pass that exam, get that interview, go for that promotion or kick-start that new business startup. Ultimately make a difference and above all else, have fun.

Continuing your journey

If you wish to continue your journey and build on the skills you have began to nurture, then sign up to this free seven-day email course to become an expert in your field. In it you will learn strategies to take everything you have learned and make it all automatic using the Tiny Habits Method, created by Dr. BJ Fogg, behaviour scientist at Stanford University, you will also get some real-life input from me.

http://improve-your-memory.memoryschool.com/

I would love to work with you personally either at a live event or in a one-to-one session. You can keep in touch at: http://memoryschool.com or follow @markchannon on Twitter.

Further reading

Bavister, S. and Vickers, A. (2010) *Essential NLP* (Teach Yourself)

Blanchard , K. (2004) *The One Minute Manager Builds High Performing Teams* (HarperCollins Enterntainment)

Covey, S. (2004) *The 7 Habits of Highly Effective People* (Simon & Schuster Ltd)

Davis, R. (2010) *The Gift of Dyslexia* (Souvenir Press)

Fisher, R. and Ury, W. (2012) *Getting to Yes: Negotiating Agreement Without Giving In* (Random House Business)

Gordon, M. (2000) *The Stanislavksy Technique* (Applause Theatre Book Publishers)

Kahneman, D. (2012) *Thinking Fast and Slow* (Penguin)

Langley, M. (2013) *The Mindfulness Workbook* (Teach Yourself)

Robbins, A. (1996) *Personal Power* (Robbins Research International)

Scheele, P. (1999) *Photoreading* (Learning Strategies Corporation)

Thompson, R. F. (1993) *The Brain: A Neuroscience Primer* (W.H. Freeman & Co. Ltd)

Yates, F. (1974) *The Art of Memory* (University of Chicago Press)

Zull, J. E. (2002) *The Art of Changing the Brain* (Stylus Publishing)

Index